SCHOLASTIC

COMIC-STRIP MATH
PROBLEM SOLVING

80 Reproducible Cartoons With Dozens and Dozens of Story
Problems That Motivate Students and Build Essential Math Skills

BY DAN GREENBERG

New York • Toronto • London • Auckland • Sydney
Mexico City • New Delhi • Hong Kong • Buenos Aires

Teaching
Resources

Previously published as *Comic-Strip Math* and *Comic-Strip Math: Mini-Story Problems*

Editor: Mela Ottaiano
Cover design by Jason Robinson.
Interior design by Grafica Inc.
Cover and interior illustrations by Jared Lee

ISBN-13 978-0-545-19571-3
ISBN-10 0-545-19571-3

TABLE OF CONTENTS

INTRODUCTION

ABOUT THIS BOOK

The purpose of this book should be clear from its title: to make math fun! The comic strips on these pages are funny. But they also have a serious job—to give students context. Math, after all, is ultimately about solving problems in a particular situation. The more interesting the situation, the more motivated most students are to pursue mathematical goals. This book provides contexts—80 of them—that students can really sink their teeth into.

Using funny characters and a whimsical point of view, the comics and companion problems on these pages explore a variety of critical mathematical topics that are specified by the National Council of Teachers of Mathematics Curriculum Standards. Topics focus on basic number operations—addition, subtraction, multiplication, and division—and cover more complex elements, such as fractions, decimals, estimation, mental math, measurement, geometry, and more.

USING THIS BOOK

Comic-Strip Math: Problem Solving can supplement your core mathematical program in many ways: as part of an interdisciplinary program that integrates reading and math; as an in-class reward for work well done; to introduce new problem-solving skills to students who are ahead of the class; or to review topics for students who need extra help.

Each activity page encourages students to apply their visual, verbal, spatial, and reasoning skills to interpret situations and solve mathematical problems.

The book is divided into 13 sections: Place Value & Rounding; Addition & Subtraction; Multiplication & Division; Mixed Operations; Fractions; Decimals; Time; Money; Measurement; Graphs; Geometry; Patterns; and Rate, Ratio, Probability & Statistics. These reflect the main skills students will focus on in a given section.

The Skills Chart (pages 6 and 7) gives an in-depth analysis of the additional skills students will use to complete each page.

The Super Challenges function as a way to extend learning—in some cases encouraging students to draw pictures or diagrams, make models, collect data, and create their own problems. All invite students to apply what they've learned in a new, unique, or more complex way.

Complete answers are on pages 88–96.

In the classroom, the cartoons can be employed in a variety of ways including:

- Whole-class participation: Students work together to solve problems.
- Small-group participation: Teams of students to find solutions on their own.
- Individually: Student can solve the problems either as work in class, homework, or as part of a self-paced study.

FINALLY . . .

The purpose of this book is to help students see math as a fun and interesting part of their real world, while using basic problem solving, critical thinking, and reasoning skills. But don't stop there. Encourage students to look for other ways to incorporate math and mathematical thinking into their own lives. Show students that the more math they learn, the more fun it becomes!

SKILLS CHART

Comic-Strip Math: Problem-Solving © 2010 by Dan Greenberg, Scholastic Teaching Resources

SKILLS CHART

7

Name: _____

PHONEY BALONEY starring Steve Hummingbird and Ant Betty

FIGURE IT OUT!

1. Write the number 6,789 out as a word: _____

_____

2. In the number 6,789, which place does the digit 8 occupy?

_____

3. In the number 6,789, which digit is in the ones' place?

_____

4. Write the number 476,789 out as a word.

_____

5. In the number 476,789, which digit is in the hundred thousands' place?

_____

6. In the number 476,789, what places does the digit 7 occupy?

_____

SUPER CHALLENGE: Round the number 12,476,789 to the nearest thousand. Now round the number 12,476,789 to the nearest million.

Name: _____

NICE HAT starring Woovis the Dog and Rudy Rabbit

> ### FIGURE IT OUT!
>
> **1.** Rudy Rabbit decides he couldn't wait 1,000 years to call. Instead, he would wait only 17 years. To the nearest ten, how many years does Rudy wait?_____

2. Suppose Rudy calls after 54 years. To the nearest ten, how many years is this?

_____

3. Suppose Rudy waits 133 years. To the nearest ten, how many years is this? To the nearest hundred?

_____

4. Suppose Rudy waits 452 years. To the nearest hundred, how many years is this? To the nearest ten?

_____

5. Suppose Rudy calls after 687 years. To the nearest hundred, how many years is this? To the nearest thousand?

_____

SUPER CHALLENGE: Rounded to the nearest hundred, a number equals 1,000. What is the smallest value that this number can have?

Name: _____

THE TREE starring Rowena Pig and Itchy Squirrel

FIGURE IT OUT!

1. The apple that hit Rowena Pig fell from a branch that is 30 feet above the ground. How far is the branch from the top of the 100-foot tree?

_____

2. Rowena's ladder reaches up to 50 feet. How many feet shorter is the ladder than the 100-foot tree?

_____

3. Starting on the ground, Itchy Squirrel climbs 20 feet up the tree. Then she stops to rest. She climbs 37 feet more and stops to rest again. How many feet did Itchy climb up the tree?

_____

4. Rowena climbs 47 feet up the tree. Then an apple falls on her. The apple fell from a branch that is 92 feet up the tree. How many feet did the apple drop before hitting Rowena?

_____

5. Itchy climbs 57 feet up the 100-foot tree. Then she climbs down 28 feet. How many feet is she from the top of the tree?

_____

SUPER CHALLENGE: Itchy is 20 feet from the top of the 100-foot tree. She jumps straight across to a second tree. Now she's 30 feet from the top of the second tree. How tall is the second tree?

Name: _____

YOU DON'T SAY starring Woovis the Dog and Moovis the Cow

FIGURE IT OUT!

1. In their comedy act, Moovis and Woovis told 7 utterly funny jokes and 4 udderly funny jokes. How many jokes did they tell in all?

_____

2. Woovis told 16 dog biscuit jokes. The audience laughed at all but 7 of them. How many dog biscuit jokes did the audience laugh at?

_____

3. Woovis and Moovis were on stage for a total of 45 minutes. Before the intermission, they were on stage for 21 minutes. How long were they on stage after the intermission?

_____

4. The Woovis and Moovis Show played for 5 nights in New York. The show played for twice as many nights in Chicago than it played in New York. How many nights did the show play in all?

_____

5. In New York, Woovis and Moovis were paid a combined total of $10 for each show. But Woovis earned $2 more for each show than Moovis earned. How much did each animal earn for each show?

_____

SUPER CHALLENGE: The Woovis and Moovis Show needs jokes. Can you help them out? Find or make up a good joke that has a math problem in it. Then write your joke and display it in class. Add pictures if you wish!

Name: _____

WHO'S GOT THE BUTTON? starring Molly Mouse and Ant Betty

They say that every 3 seconds, somebody somewhere loses a button.

Good gracious!

You'd think that person would learn to keep track of his buttons after a while.

FIGURE IT OUT!

1. If a button is lost every 3 seconds, how many buttons are lost in 60 seconds?

_____

2. Ant Betty finds some buttons. She gives 7 buttons to each of her 8 nieces. How many buttons did she find?

_____

3. Molly Mouse organizes 6 groups of mice to look for lost buttons. Each group has 5 mice. How many mice are there in all?

_____

4. One group of mice finds many buttons and they put them into 9 bags. Each bag contains 14 buttons. How many buttons did the mice find?

_____

5. A second group of mice collects 20 bags containing a total of 160 buttons. Each bag contains the same number of buttons. How many buttons are in each bag?

_____

SUPER CHALLENGE: Suppose 20 mice want to form teams with an equal number of mice on each team. How many different-size teams can they form?

Name: _____

PAIN IN THE NECK starring Dr. Woovis and Rowena Pig

FIGURE IT OUT!

1. Dr. Woovis wants Rowena Pig to take 2 red pills a day for 10 days. How many red pills will Rowena take in all?_____

2. Red pills come in two different-size bottles. The large bottle contains 100 pills. The small bottle contains 40 pills. Which has more pills—1 large bottle or 3 small bottles?

_____

3. Harry Horse needs to take 6 blue pills a day. If a bottle of blue pills has 84 pills, how many days will it last?

_____

4. How many days will a bottle of 294 blue pills last if a patient takes 6 blue pills per day?

_____

5. Rudy Rabbit needs to take 9 green pills a day for 2 weeks. How many green pills will he take in all?

_____

SUPER CHALLENGE: Dr. Woovis wants Squirmy Worm to take 8 purple pills a day for 3 weeks, then 6 purple pills a day for the following 2 weeks. How many purple pills will Squirmy take in all?

Name: _____

RABBIT FEET starring Woovis the Dog and Rudy Rabbit

> Hey Woovis, when do rabbits have 20 feet?

> I don't know, Rudy. When?

> When there are 5 rabbits. Get it?

FIGURE IT OUT!

1. A rabbit has 4 feet. How many feet do 4 rabbits have?

   _____

2. A group of rabbits has a total of 24 feet. How many rabbits are in the group?

   _____

3. A starfish has 5 legs. Four starfish were doing underwater cartwheels. How many legs were doing cartwheels?

   _____

4. A beetle has 6 legs. A total of 22 beetles bought basketball sneakers. How many sneakers did they buy?

   _____

5. A group of eight-legged spiders with a total of 48 legs is walking with a group of rabbits that have a total of 12 legs. How many animals are walking?

   _____

6. Two spiders and 1 rabbit leave the walking group. Five people join the group. How many legs are walking in all?

   _____

SUPER CHALLENGE: Draw a cartoon that shows how you solved one of the problems on this page.

Comic-Strip Math: Problem-Solving © 2010 by Dan Greenberg, Scholastic Teaching Resources

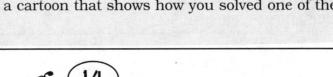

Name: _____

SEVEN-KERPLUNK! starring Woovis the Dog and Wendy Spider

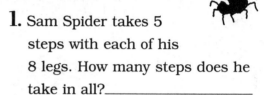

FIGURE IT OUT!

1. Sam Spider takes 5 steps with each of his 8 legs. How many steps does he take in all?_____

2. Sharon Spider takes 72 steps in all. How many steps does she take with each of her 8 legs?

_____

3. Susan Spider takes 14 steps with each of her 8 legs. How many more steps does she take than Sharon in problem 2?

_____

4. Mike Spider takes 7 rounds of steps. Then he takes 23 rounds of steps. How many steps did he take in all?

_____

5. Wendy Spider has a cast on her broken leg. She takes 7 steps with her broken leg. In total, how many steps does she take with her other 7 legs?

_____

SUPER CHALLENGE: Gary Grasshopper takes 26 steps with each of his 6 legs. Does he take more steps than the total number of steps taken by all the spiders in problems 1, 2, 3?

Name: _____

STAIRWAY TO THE TOP starring Squirmy Worm and Ant Betty

FIGURE IT OUT!

1. Each staircase had 9 steps. How many staircases did Ant Betty climb to get from the 1st floor to the 3rd floor? How many steps did she climb? _____

2. Ant Betty went from the 3rd floor to the 8th floor. How many steps did she climb?

_____

3. Squirmy started on the 2nd floor and walked up 27 steps. What floor did he end up on?

_____

4. Squirmy walked from the basement to the 6th floor. How many steps did he walk up?

_____

5. Squirmy walked from the 8th floor to the basement. How many steps did he descend?

_____

6. Ant Betty started on the 2nd floor and walked up 45 steps. Then she walked down 18 steps. On which floor did she end up?

_____

SUPER CHALLENGE: Suppose the building had 7-step staircases on each floor instead of 9. How would that change your answer to problem 2?

Name: _____

CAMOUFLAGE starring Woovis the Dog and Moovis the Cow

FIGURE IT OUT!

1. A total of 32 cows hid in the tops of 4 maple trees. Each tree held the same number of cows. How many cows were in each tree? _____

2. Two trees held an equal number of birds and cows. There were a total of 24 birds and 8 cows. How many animals were in each tree?

_____

3. Forty-eight cows hid in the tops of some trees. Each tree held 8 cows. How many trees were there in all?

_____

4. There were 5 trees in a yard. If 7 cows hid in each tree, how many cows were there in all?

_____

5. A total of 54 cows found 9 trees to hide in. The same number of cows hid in each tree. How many cows hid in each tree?

_____

SUPER CHALLENGE: Going to sleep, Woovis counted 96 cows jumping over a fence in 6 minutes. If he counted an equal number of cows each minute, how many cows jumped the fence each minute?

Name: _____

GOLF PRO starring Woovis the Dog and Tiger Jones

FIGURE IT OUT!

1. The Tiger Jones Golf Tournament features $100,000 in prize money. If 8 players split the prize money equally, how much will each player win? _____

2. How much in prize money will each player win if they split $100,000 equally among 16 players?

_____

3. How many players would there be if they split up the $100,000 equally and each player got $5,000?

_____

4. Last year the $100,000 prize money was split among the top 3 players only. The winner got half of the money, and the remaining 2 players split up the rest equally. How much did each player get?

_____

5. This year's 3rd place finisher won 2.25 as much prize money as the 4th place finisher. If the 3rd place finisher got $9,000, how much did the 4th place finisher win?

_____

SUPER CHALLENGE: Create a prize money scheme in which the winner gets twice as much as the 2nd place finisher. The 2nd place finisher gets twice as much as the 3rd place finisher. The 3rd place finisher gets twice as much as the 4th place finisher, and so on. How much does each player win?

Comic-Strip Math: Problem-Solving © 2010 by Dan Greenberg, Scholastic Teaching Resources

Name: _____

CARROT SOUP starring Squirmy Worm and Rudy Rabbit

This soup must be worth a fortune.

Why do you say that?

Because it's made with 14 carrots.

Wow.

FIGURE IT OUT!

1. Rudy has 58 carrots. How many pots of 14-carrot soup could he make? How many leftover carrots would he have? _____

2. How many carrots does Rudy need to make 12 pots of 14-carrot soup? How many carrots does he need to make 16 pots of 7-carrot soup?

_____

3. How many pots of 14-carrot soup can Rudy make with 126 carrots? How many pots of 7-carrot soup can Rudy make with the same number of carrots?

_____

4. How many pots of 7-carrot soup can Rudy make with 100 carrots? How many carrots will be left over?

_____

5. Rudy has 63 carrots. How many pots of 7-carrot soup can he make? How many pots of 14-carrot soup? How many carrots will be left over?

_____

SUPER CHALLENGE: Make a table that shows how many pots of 7-carrot soup and 14-carrot soup Rudy can make with 42 carrots, 56 carrots, 70 carrots, and 84 carrots. What pattern do you see? How could you use the pattern to solve other soup problems?

Name: _____

HOOP DREAMS starring Molly Mouse, Rudy Rabbit, and Judy Frog

FIGURE IT OUT!

1. If Michael Jordan can jump 3 feet off the ground and Judy Frog can jump 2 times as high wearing her basketball sneakers, how high can Judy jump?_____

2. Wearing her new Super Springy sneakers, Judy can jump 3 times as high as with her regular basketball sneakers. How high can Judy jump with her new sneakers?

_____

3. In 6 games, Judy scored 17, 13, 21, 16, 9, and 20 points. How many points did she score in all?

_____

4. Judy's team played 9 games. The team scored 50 points in each game. How many points did the team score in all the games?

_____

5. Judy scored 30 points in the championship game. She scored three 3-point baskets and five 1-point baskets. How many 2-point baskets did she score?

_____

SUPER CHALLENGE: In the championship game, Judy scored the highest with 30 points, which is 6 more than the second-highest scorer. The second-highest scorer scored 6 more points than the third-highest scorer, and so on for all five players on the team. How many points did the team score in all?

Name: _____

THE SQUIRM-ULATOR starring Squirmy Worm and Moovis the Cow

FIGURE IT OUT!

1. Help out Squirmy Worm. What do you get when you multiply 6 by 7, then subtract 13? Use a calculator to check the answer.

_____

2. Squirmy multiplies 8 by 5, then divides the product by 4. What is the answer?

_____

3. Moovis the Cow multiplies 11 by 14. Then she divides the product by 7. What is the answer?

_____

4. Multiply the number of days there are in a week by 12. Subtract 24. What is the answer?

_____

5. How old are you? Multiply your age in years by 17. Then add or subtract to get a total of 200. What number did you add or subtract?

_____

SUPER CHALLENGE: On which day of the month were you born? Multiply this number by 3. Is the product higher than 100?

Name: _____

A FAMILIAR FACE starring Monica Bear and Squirmy Worm

FIGURE IT OUT!

1. Squirmy Worm has 100 brothers. Forty of them are students at Worm University. How many brothers are not students at Worm U?

_____

2. Twenty of Squirmy's brothers will graduate from Worm University. Squirmy plans to give each brother 4 pebbles as gifts. How many pebbles does he need in all?

_____

3. Some of Squirmy's sisters will also graduate from Worm U. He plans to give them twigs as gifts. Squirmy has 150 twigs. Each sister will get 5 twigs. How many sisters will graduate?

_____

4. Two worms gave speeches at the Worm University graduation. One speech lasted 68 minutes. The other speech was 13 minutes longer. How many minutes was the second speech?

_____

5. A total of 1,056 worms will graduate from Worm U. Of those, 356 plan to become soil farmers and 119 plan to work in the sanitation business. The rest plan to become lawyers. How many worms plan to be lawyers?

_____

SUPER CHALLENGE: Do more or less than half of the graduating class in problem 5 want to become lawyers?

Name: _____

THE DAY OF THE DENTIST starring Tiger Jones and Wendy Spider

FIGURE IT OUT!

1. Tiger had 7 teeth when he was a baby. Now he has 3 times as many teeth. How many teeth does Tiger have now?_____

2. Tiger Jones has 11 more stripes than Tiger Smith. Tiger Jones has 46 stripes. How many stripes does Tiger Smith have?

_____

3. Tiger Brown has 14 fewer stripes than Tiger Jones. Does Tiger Brown have fewer stripes than Tiger Smith?

_____

4. Tiger's dentist saw twice as many patients today as she saw yesterday. She saw 12 patients today. How many did she see yesterday?

_____

5. A spider has 8 legs. A group of spiders has a total of 32 legs. How many spiders are there in the group?

_____

SUPER CHALLENGE: Tiger Jones played for 8 hours on Saturday. That is twice as long as he played on Friday and half as long as he played on Sunday. How much longer did he play on Sunday than he played on Friday?

Name: _____

POLITICS starring Woovis the Dog and Fangella the Snake

Who lives in the White House, is elected every 4 years, and speaks with a forked tongue?

I don't know. Who?

The President of the United Snakes.

FIGURE IT OUT!

1. One term for the President of the United Snakes lasts for 4 years. How many years does a President serve if he or she serves 3 terms?

_____

2. Franklin Delano Rattles was President of the United Snakes for 16 years. How many terms did he serve?

_____

3. Snake representatives serve 2-year terms. Fangella was in Snake Congress from 1984 until 1996. How many terms did she serve?

_____

4. Snake Congress has 500 members. More than half of the representatives must vote for a law to get it passed. At least how many members have to vote for a law to get it passed?

_____

5. One law got 12 more votes than half of all the snake representatives. How many votes did the law get?

_____

SUPER CHALLENGE: To change the Snake Constitution, 100 more than half the representatives must vote to make a change. How many votes are needed to change the Snake Constitution?

Name: _____

MIDNIGHT IN THE BARN starring Molly Mouse and Harry Horse

FIGURE IT OUT!

1. There are 24 horse stalls in the barn. One half of the stalls had horses in them when Molly Mouse came running by last night. How many stalls had horses?

_____

2. Each of 18 horses eats $\frac{2}{3}$ of a bale of hay. How many bales do 18 horses eat?

_____

3. Each cow eats $\frac{2}{5}$ bale of hay every morning. How many bales do 10 cows eat?

_____

4. Half of the chickens in the barn laid an egg. Half of those eggs were white. What fraction of all the chickens laid a white egg?

_____

5. Four sevenths of the pigs eat at a trough. Two sevenths of the pigs roll in the mud. There are 28 pigs. How many pigs eat in the trough and roll in the mud?

_____

SUPER CHALLENGE: There are 50 horses in the corral. Three fifths of the horses wear saddles. Half of the horses wearing saddles have a rider. What fraction of all the horses in the corral has a rider? Write your answer in simplest form.

Name: _____

WHITE SOCKS, BLACK SOCKS starring Rowena Pig and Judy Frog

FIGURE IT OUT!

1. Rowena Pig is wearing 1 white sock and 1 black sock. What fraction of the socks she's wearing is white? What fraction is black?

_____

2. Rowena puts 7 socks in the washing machine. Four of them are black and 3 are white. What fraction of the socks is black? What fraction is white?

_____

3. Rowena hangs 8 socks out to dry. Two of the socks are black and 6 are white. What fraction is black? Write your answer in simplest form.

_____

4. Judy Frog brings 6 socks on a trip. One third of the socks are red. The rest are green. How many socks are red? How many are green?

_____

5. Six out of 10 socks are blue. The rest are red. What fraction of the socks is red? Write your answer in simplest form.

_____

SUPER CHALLENGE: Judy has 12 socks. One third of them are white. One fourth of them are red. The rest are yellow. How many socks are yellow? How many socks are white and red?

Comic-Strip Math: Problem-Solving © 2010 by Dan Greenberg, Scholastic Teaching Resources

Name: _____

FRIENDSHIP starring Ed and Fred, the Singing Giraffe Brothers

FIGURE IT OUT!

1. Ant Betty is Ed's friend. To talk to Ed, she has to climb up his 12-foot-long neck. Betty climbs 3 feet up Ed's neck. What fraction is 3 of 12? Write the fraction in simplest form.

_____

2. Ant Betty climbs 6 feet up Ed's 12-foot neck. What fraction is 6 of 12? Write the fraction in simplest form.

_____

3. What fraction of Ed's 12-foot neck did Betty climb after going 8 feet? Write the fraction in simplest form.

_____

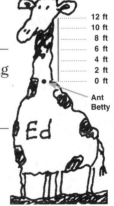

4. How many feet must Ant Betty climb to cover $\frac{3}{4}$ of Ed's 12-foot neck?

_____

5. Ant Betty climbs $\frac{5}{6}$ of the way up Ed's neck. How many more feet does she need to go to reach the top of his neck?

_____

SUPER CHALLENGE: Fred has a 14-foot neck. How many feet would you have to climb to get halfway up Fred's neck? How many feet would you have to climb to get halfway up Ed's neck? Which distance is greater? How much greater?

Name: _____

AT THE MOVIES starring Woovis the Dog and Judy Frog

FIGURE IT OUT!

1. Mint gum runs out of flavor after $7\frac{3}{5}$ minutes. Suppose Woovis the Dog can make gum flavor last $3\frac{1}{5}$ minutes longer. How long will the gum's flavor last?

_____

2. Woovis eats one jelly bean in $1\frac{2}{3}$ minutes. He eats a milk ball in $1\frac{1}{6}$ minutes. How long does it take him to eat the jelly bean and milk ball?

_____

3. A lollipop lasts 12 minutes. After $6\frac{1}{2}$ minutes, how many more minutes will the pop last?

_____

4. Woovis sees two movie previews. One lasts $6\frac{3}{4}$ minutes and the other lasts $4\frac{5}{8}$ minutes. How long do both previews last?

_____

5. Judy Frog comes in $12\frac{1}{2}$ minutes late to *Revenge of the Flies* and stays until the end. The movie runs for 70 minutes. How much of the movie does she see?

_____

SUPER CHALLENGE: Woovis starts eating his popcorn when *Frogs, Dogs, and Choo-Choo Trains* begins. The movie runs for $72\frac{1}{4}$ minutes. Woovis's popcorn lasts for $48\frac{1}{2}$ minutes. How many minutes of the movie will be left when Woovis finishes his popcorn?

Comic-Strip Math: Problem-Solving © 2010 by Dan Greenberg, Scholastic Teaching Resources

HAT HOLE starring Moovis the Cow and Harry Horse

FIGURE IT OUT!

1. Harry Horse's hat measures $14\frac{5}{8}$ inches around. Woovis the Dog's hat measures $6\frac{3}{8}$ inches around. How much larger is Harry's hat?

_____

2. Woovis puts 2 snowballs into Harry's hat. Each snowball weighs $3\frac{2}{3}$ ounces. How much do the 2 snowballs weigh?

_____

3. Harry splits a 9-ounce snowball into 4 equal-size pieces. How much does each piece weigh?

_____

4. Moovis the Cow splits an $8\frac{1}{3}$-ounce snowball into 5 equal-size pieces. How much does each piece weigh?

_____

5. Compare the pieces in problems 3 and 4. Which pieces weigh more? How much more do they weigh?

_____

SUPER CHALLENGE: Suppose you fill a hat with 20 ounces of lemonade. Then you pour the lemonade evenly into either 5 blue cups or 6 red cups. Which would have more lemonade—a blue cup or a red cup?

Name: _____

BEACH DAY starring Woovis the Dog and Monica Bear

FIGURE IT OUT!

1. Woovis the Dog drives Monica Bear $\frac{3}{5}$ of a mile to the beach. A cab ride costs 50¢ per mile. How much did the ride cost?_____

2. At the beach, Woovis picks up a chicken. He drives $\frac{3}{5}$ of a mile down Shore Road. Then he turns right on Coop Street and drives $\frac{2}{5}$ of a mile to a hen house. How far did he drive in all? How much did the ride cost?

_____

3. Woovis drives a skunk $\frac{9}{10}$ of a mile to a skunk den. Then he drives a cat $\frac{4}{5}$ of a mile to a milk bar. Which animal did Woovis drive farther? How much farther?

_____

4. Woovis drives $\frac{3}{8}$ of a mile to the park. Then he drives $\frac{1}{2}$ of a mile to the zoo. How far does he drive in all?

_____

5. The Surf Hotel, Beach Hotel, and Walt's Drive-In are all on the same road. Surf Hotel and Beach Hotel are 1 mile apart. Walt's Drive-In is between the two hotels. It is $\frac{3}{10}$ of a mile from Beach Hotel. How far is the drive-in from Surf Hotel?

_____

SUPER CHALLENGE: Woovis drives $\frac{5}{9}$ of a mile to Beach Hotel. Then he drives $\frac{1}{6}$ of a mile to the beach. How far does he drive in all?

Name: _____

BASEBALL FEVER starring Woovis the Dog and Judy Frog

FIGURE IT OUT!

1. Judy caught 5 out of 10 flies. Write this as a fraction in simplest form.

   _____

2. In a baseball game, 8 balls were hit. Judy caught 6 of the balls. What fraction did Judy catch? Write your answer in simplest form.

   _____

3. After the game, Judy caught half of the 12 insect flies that came past. How many flies did she catch?

   _____

4. Judy caught 5 out of 15 grounders that were hit to her in a baseball game. What fraction of groundballs did she catch? Write your answer in simplest form.

   _____

5. In the grass, Judy caught 6 out of 18 insects. What fraction of insects did she catch? Write your answer in simplest form.

   _____

SUPER CHALLENGE: Woovis got a hit 9 out of 30 times. What fraction of the time did Woovis <u>not</u> get a hit? Write your answer in simplest form.

Name: _____

DOCTOR KNOWS BEST starring Dr. Woovis and Judy Frog

FIGURE IT OUT!

1. Judy had a full mug of cocoa. She drank $\frac{1}{3}$ of the cocoa in the mug. What fraction of cocoa was left?_____

2. Dr. Woovis drank $\frac{1}{6}$ of a mug of cocoa. After lunch, he drank another $\frac{3}{6}$ of a mug. What fraction of the mug did he drink in all? Write your answer in simplest form.

_____

3. Judy poured $\frac{3}{8}$ of a mug of cocoa into a mug that was already $\frac{1}{8}$ full. What fraction of a mug was filled with cocoa? Write your answer in simplest form.

_____

4. Fangella had a full mug of tea. She spilled $\frac{8}{12}$ of the tea. What fraction of tea was left in the mug? Write your answer in simplest form.

_____

5. A glass is $\frac{1}{6}$ full of water. What fraction of a full glass do you need to add to fill the glass halfway?

_____

SUPER CHALLENGE: A ladle holds $\frac{3}{8}$ of a cup of water. How many ladles can you add together before you have more than 2 cups of water? What fraction of a cup will you have left over?

NEW BOOTS starring Woovis the Dog, and Sal and Al Gator

FIGURE IT OUT!

1. Sal grew 2 inches in March and $1\frac{1}{4}$ inches in April. How many total inches did she grow in these two months?_____

_____

2. Sal grew $1\frac{3}{4}$ inches in May. How much more did she grow in May than in April? Write your answer in simplest form.

_____

3. How many total inches did Sal grow in March, April, and May?

_____

4. How many more inches did Sal grow in March than in April?

_____

5. Sal grew $\frac{3}{8}$ of an inch in June. How many total inches did she grow in May and June?

_____

6. How many more inches did Sal grow in May than in June?

_____

SUPER CHALLENGE: Measure your own growth rate over the year. What was the average number of inches you grew each month?

Name: _____

STUBBED starring Squirmy Worm and Wendy Spider

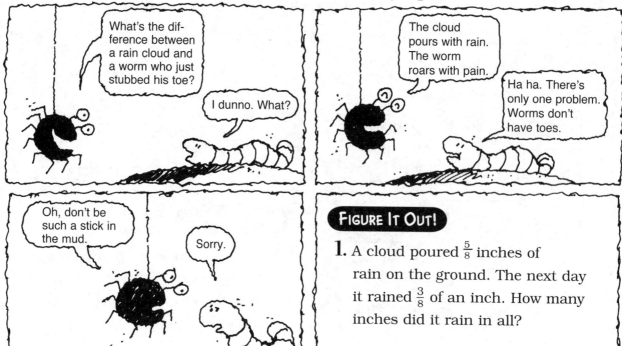

What's the difference between a rain cloud and a worm who just stubbed his toe?

I dunno. What?

The cloud pours with rain. The worm roars with pain.

Ha ha. There's only one problem. Worms don't have toes.

Oh, don't be such a stick in the mud.

Sorry.

FIGURE IT OUT!

1. A cloud poured $\frac{5}{8}$ inches of rain on the ground. The next day it rained $\frac{3}{8}$ of an inch. How many inches did it rain in all?

_____

2. In problem 1, how many more inches did it rain on the first day than on the second day?

_____

3. Wendy spun a thread of silk $4\frac{1}{2}$ inches long. Then she tied it to a second thread $2\frac{3}{4}$ inches long. What was the total length of the two threads?

_____

4. Squirmy measures $2\frac{1}{8}$ inches in length. Squirmy's Uncle Walter measures 4 inches. How much longer is Uncle Walter than Squirmy?

_____

5. Suppose Squirmy grows $\frac{2}{3}$ of an inch this year. How long will he be?

_____

SUPER CHALLENGE: Write down your height and the heights of your classmates. Then add the numbers together. What is the total height of your class?

Name: _____

DANCE FEVER starring Woovis the Dog and Rowena Pig

FIGURE IT OUT!

1. Woovis danced with $\frac{3}{4}$ of the 24 dogs at the dance. How many dogs did Woovis dance with?

_____

2. Rowena danced with $\frac{4}{5}$ of the 20 pigs at the dance. How many pigs did Rowena dance with?

_____

3. Who danced with more partners, Woovis or Rowena? How many more?

_____

4. Half of the partners Rowena danced with were clumsy. How many were not clumsy?

_____

5. What fraction of all of the pigs and dogs did Woovis and Rowena dance with?

_____

SUPER CHALLENGE: Woovis and Harry the Horse are males. Rowena and Fangella the Snake are females. How many different dance couples can the 4 of them form where 1 partner is male and 1 partner is female?

Name: _____

WHAT'S HOPPIN'? starring Judy Frog and Rudy Rabbit

FIGURE IT OUT!

1. Rudy climbed to the 50th floor of the 100-story building. What fraction of the way to the top did he climb? _____

2. What floor does Rudy need to climb to so he is $\frac{1}{4}$ of the way to the top of the 100-story building?

_____

3. What fraction of the way to the top of the 100-story building is the 20th floor?

_____

4. What floor does Rudy need to climb to so he is $\frac{2}{5}$ of the way to the top of the building?

_____

5. Rudy is on the 68th floor. How many floors does he have to climb so he is $\frac{3}{4}$ of the way to the top of the building?

_____

6. Is the 30th floor less than $\frac{1}{3}$ of the way to the top of the building? Explain.

_____

SUPER CHALLENGE: Which would be closer to the top: Being on the 60th floor of a 100-story building or being on the 60th floor of an 80-story building? Explain.

Name: _____

LEFTOVERS starring Woovis the Dog and Fangella the Snake

FIGURE IT OUT!

1. There are 12 snakes in a diner. Five of the snakes order soup. Write a fraction that shows how many snakes order soup.

_____

2. Write a fraction that shows how many snakes in the diner did not order soup.

_____

3. There are 10 rabbits in the diner. Five of the rabbits order carrot cake. What fraction of the rabbits ordered cake?

_____

4. Nine pigs come into the diner. One third of the pigs order slop. How many pigs order slop?

_____

5. Write a fraction that shows how many pigs did not order slop. Write your answer in simplest form.

_____

SUPER CHALLENGE: Three-quarters of the snakes in the diner and $\frac{2}{5}$ of the rabbits order ice cream. How many snakes and rabbits order ice cream?

Name: _____

DUET starring Ed and Fred, the Singing Giraffe Brothers

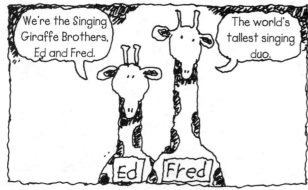

FIGURE IT OUT!

1. Ed and Fred are the Singing Giraffe Brothers. Ed is 24.2 feet tall. Fred is 26.5 feet tall. How much taller is Fred?_____

2. Fred stands next to a 30-foot tree. How many feet taller is the tree than Fred?

_____

3. Ed stands on a 6.3-foot platform. The platform is next to a 30-foot tree. How much higher is Ed than the tree?

_____

4. Fred is standing on the same 6.3-foot platform. How much higher is Fred than the 30-foot-tall tree?

_____

5. Jed is the third of the Singing Giraffe Brothers. He is only 18.6 feet tall. Jed wears elevator boots to make himself as tall as Ed. How high are Jed's elevator boots?

_____

SUPER CHALLENGE: Ed, Fred, and Jed want to wear elevator boots so they can all be the same height. If they all want to appear to be 32 feet in height, how tall should each pair of boots be?

Name: _____

THE LADDER starring Judy Frog and Chuck Mantis

FIGURE IT OUT!

1. Judy Frog climbs up 3 steps of the ladder. If each step is 0.4 meters apart, how high is Judy off the ground? _____

_____

2. Judy climbs up 16 steps of the ladder. How many meters off the ground is she?

_____

3. Chuck Mantis climbs the ladder to a height of 8 meters. If each step has a height of 0.4 meters, how many steps does he climb?

_____

4. Judy climbs 50 steps up the ladder. How many meters does she climb?

_____

5. Which is higher—60 steps of the ladder or 25 meters? How much higher?

_____

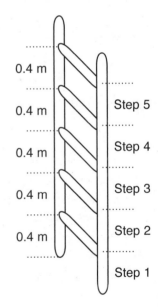

0.4 m

0.4 m   Step 5

0.4 m   Step 4

0.4 m   Step 3

0.4 m   Step 2

Step 1

SUPER CHALLENGE: A ladder is 100 meters high. Each step is 0.4 meters apart. How many steps does the ladder have?

Name: _____

THE PICNIC starring Rowena Pig and Squirmy Worm

Doggone it! I wish we had brought the TV with us on this picnic.

Why?

'Cause that's where I left the picnic basket. On top of the TV!

FIGURE IT OUT!

1. The picnic basket weighs 11.4 pounds. The TV weighs 20 pounds. How much more does the TV weigh?_____

2. The picnic basket will hold 8 pounds of food. How many 0.8-pound sandwiches will it hold?

_____

3. Which weighs more—a 0.8-pound tuna sandwich or a 0.26-pound cheese sandwich? How much more?

_____

4. Suppose Rowena Pig makes lunch bags that include a 0.8-pound sandwich and a 0.18-pound pickle. How much will each lunch bag weigh? Rowena makes 9 lunch bags. What is the total weight of all the lunches?

_____

5. There are 3 kinds of lunch boxes. The first weighs 1.6 pounds. The second weighs 2.2 pounds. The third weighs 2.5 pounds. Rowena wants to bring 3 lunch boxes that weigh exactly 6 pounds. Which combination of lunch boxes should she bring?

_____

SUPER CHALLENGE: Using the lunch boxes in problem 5, find three more ways to fill the picnic basket with 3 lunch boxes without going over the 6-pound limit.

Name: _____

THE GREAT ESCAPE starring Woovis the Dog and Rowena Pig

FIGURE IT OUT!

1. Woovis the Dog can escape from a bolt lock in 0.75 minutes. It takes him 0.4 minutes longer to escape from a key lock. How long does it take Woovis to escape from a key lock?

_____

2. It takes Woovis 1.8 minutes to escape from a combination lock. How long will it take him to escape from 3 combination locks in a row?

_____

Woovis's Escape Times

Combination Lock: 1.8 minutes

Bolt Lock: 0.75 minutes

Key Lock: _____ minutes

3. How long will it take Woovis to escape from 1 bolt lock, 3 key locks, and 4 combination locks?

_____

4. In the Underwater Trick, Woovis can hold his breath underwater for 6 minutes. How many bolt locks can he unlock in this time?

_____

5. How many key locks can Woovis unlock in 9.2 minutes?

_____

SUPER CHALLENGE: How many bolt locks can Woovis unlock in exactly 24 minutes?

Name: _____

WRESTLE-MANIA starring Monica Bear and Rudy Rabbit

FIGURE IT OUT!

1. At the weigh-in, Monica Bear weighs 452.2 pounds. Rudy Rabbit weighs in at 3.8 pounds. How much more does Monica weigh?

_____

2. If Rudy weighs 3.8 pounds, how many pounds would he need to gain to wrestle in the heavyweight division of 275 pounds or more?

_____

3. How many pounds heavier is Monica than the minimum weight for the heavyweight division?

_____

4. Woovis the Dog weighs 41.8 pounds. How many times heavier is Woovis than Rudy?

_____

5. How many times heavier is Monica than Rudy?

_____

SUPER CHALLENGE: Does Monica weigh more than 10 times as much as Woovis? About how many times heavier is Monica than Woovis?

Comic-Strip Math: Problem-Solving © 2010 by Dan Greenberg, Scholastic Teaching Resources

Name: _____

THE MOLLY MOUSE SHOW starring Molly Mouse and Woovis the Dog

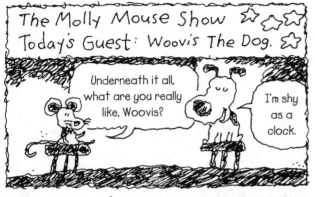

FIGURE IT OUT!

1. At 12 noon, the alarm on a clock is set to go off in 30 minutes. Where will the hands of the clock be when the alarm goes off? What number will be covered?_____

2. At 12:00, the minute hand and the hour hand line up at exactly the same place on a clock. The alarm is set to go off the next time the two hands line up in exactly the same place. What time will it be when the alarm goes off?

_____

3. An alarm is set to ring every 30 minutes starting at 2:00. When will it ring between 2:00 and 4:30?

_____

4. An alarm is set to ring every hour and a half beginning at 11:00. Will the alarm ring at 2:30 or 3:30?

_____

5. An alarm rings every 12 minutes starting at 12:00. When will it ring between 12:00 and 2:00?

_____

SUPER CHALLENGE: An alarm is set to ring every 20 minutes starting at 12:00. How many times will the alarm ring from 12:00 and 7:00?

Name: _____

GOT THE TIME? starring Rudy Rabbit and Harry Horse

FIGURE IT OUT!

1. The time on Harry Horse's first watch reads 11:30. What time is it on the second watch?

_____

2. Suppose Harry's first watch is 1 hour ahead of the second watch. The second watch reads 8:00. What time is it on Harry's first watch?

_____

3. The time on a clock is 5:08. What time will it be in 17 minutes? What time will it be in 45 minutes?

_____

4. The time on a clock is 11:30. What time will it be in 35 minutes? What time will it be in 1 hour and 15 minutes?

_____

5. The time on a clock is 2:37. What time will it be in 4 hours and 14 minutes? What time will it be in 9 hours and 23 minutes?

_____

SUPER CHALLENGE: The time on a clock is 3:22. What time was it 24 minutes earlier? What time was it 56 minutes earlier?

Name: _____

LATE TO WORK starring Judy Frog and Sal and Al Gator

FIGURE IT OUT!

1. Judy slept from 10 p.m. Saturday to 8 a.m. Sunday. How many hours did she sleep in all?

_____

2. Judy normally goes to bed at 9 p.m. and wakes up at 6:30 a.m. How many hours of sleep is that?

_____

3. One night Judy stays up late and goes to bed at 10:30 p.m. What time should she wake up the next day to get her normal amount of sleep?

_____

4. Al Gator normally goes to bed at 9:30 p.m. and gets up at 8:30 a.m. On Wednesday, Al went to bed an hour later and got up an hour earlier Thursday morning. How many hours did he sleep?

_____

5. On Thursday, Al went to sleep an hour and a half earlier than normal. He got up an hour and a half earlier than his normal wake-up time. How many hours did he sleep?

_____

SUPER CHALLENGE: Judy needs 2 hours to get ready for work. If her clock is 1 hour fast, for what time should she set her alarm to arrive at work at an actual time of 8:30 a.m.?

Name: _____

BURNT CAKE starring Judy Frog and Steve Hummingbird

FIGURE IT OUT!

1. Judy put her cake in the oven at 6:45 p.m. That cake started to burn at 8:30 p.m. How long was the cake in the oven before it began burning? _____

2. Judy's cakes all take the same time to burn. The next day, Judy puts another cake in the over at 12:25 p.m. What time will the cake begin to burn?

_____

3. Judy baked an apple pie for $1\frac{1}{3}$ hours. If she started baking the pie at 9:30 a.m., when was it done?

_____

4. An apple pie bakes for $1\frac{1}{3}$ hours. When will the pie be done if it is put in the oven at 11:40 a.m.?

_____

5. Judy started work at 8:30 a.m. She worked for $8\frac{3}{4}$ hours. What time did she finish work?

_____

SUPER CHALLENGE: Find a cookie recipe in a cookbook. How long will it take to make 3 batches of cookies using the cookbook recipe?

Name: _____

TAXI, TAXI! starring Rowena Pig and Squirmy Worm

FIGURE IT OUT!

1. The movie *Pigs Have More Fun* starts at 11:15 and lasts 1 hour and 30 minutes. What time will the movie end?_____

2. The theater showing *Pigs Have More Fun* runs the movie throughout the day. Each show starts 15 minutes after the previous one ends. If the first show starts at 11:15 a.m., what time does the second one begin?

_____

3. What time does the third showing start? If Woovis arrives at 3 p.m. will he be in time to see the beginning of the movie?

_____

4. Harry the Horse wants to see the movie after 6 p.m. But he needs to be home by 8:30 p.m. Can he see the movie?

_____

5. Between 11:15 a.m. and 9:45 p.m., how many times is *Pigs Have More Fun* shown at the beginning of an hour?

_____

SUPER CHALLENGE: This theater also shows the movie *Citizen Pig* every 2 hours and 15 minutes starting at 11:30 a.m. What time will *Citizen Pig* begin between 3 p.m. and 5 p.m.?

Name: _____

NIGHT SCHOOL starring Woovis the Dog and Moovis the Cow

THE MOOVIS AND WOOVIS SHOW

I'm Moovis. He's Woovis.

Hey Moovis, I hear you're going to night school.

That's 100 percent correct.

Why night school?

I want to learn how to read in the dark.

Sigh.

FIGURE IT OUT!

1. In 1 hour, Moovis read 43 pages of a 212-page book called *The Big Moo*. Estimate how many total hours it will take her to finish the book. _____

2. Woovis read 29 pages of *The Big Moo* in 1 hour. Remember, the book has 212 pages. About how many total hours will it take him to finish the book?

_____

3. Woovis can read *Moo Over Miami* twice as fast as he can read *The Big Moo*. About how many pages of *Moo Over Miami* can he read in 6 hours?

_____

4. *Moo Over Miami* has 532 pages. About how many hours will it take Woovis to read the entire book if he reads at the same rate he read in problem 3?

_____

5. Moovis read 48 pages of *Moo Over Miami* in one hour. About how many hours will it take her to read the entire 532-page book?

_____

The Moo Lagoon **$5.95**

COW FOR A DAY **$3.75**

THE BIG MOO **$2.50**

Moo Over Miami **$1.95**

SUPER CHALLENGE: Moovis wants to buy 2 books. Which books can she buy for under $5? For under $6? For under $10?

Comic-Strip Math: Problem-Solving © 2010 by Dan Greenberg, Scholastic Teaching Resources

Name: _____

KEEPING COOL starring Chuck Mantis and Squirmy Worm

FIGURE IT OUT!

1. Chuck Mantis buys an air conditioner on January 1. The air conditioner has a 30-day guarantee. On what day will the guarantee expire?

_____

2. Squirmy Worm goes grocery shopping every 3rd day. If he shops on January 11, what are the next two dates he will go shopping again?

_____

3. Chuck shops every 6th day. If he shops on a Saturday, on what day of the week will he go shopping next?

_____

4. Woovis the Dog goes shopping on January 20. He goes shopping 12 days later. On what date does he go shopping again?

_____

5. How many days are there from January 15 to February 12?

_____

SUPER CHALLENGE: Rowena Pig goes grocery shopping every 3rd day. If she shops on Saturday, January 1, on what date will she shop on a Saturday again?

Name: _____

FUNNY MONEY starring Rudy Rabbit and Woovis the Dog

FIGURE IT OUT!

1. Rudy Rabbit has two $10 bills. How much money does he have?

_____

Use mental math to solve each problem.

2. What is the value of four $10 bills? Six $10 bills? Ten $10 bills?

_____

3. What is the value of eight $100 bills? Sixteen $100 bills? Twenty-five $100 bills?

_____

4. Rudy has $400. How many $100 bills equal $400? How many $10 bills equal $400?

_____

5. Rudy has $5,700. How many $100 bills could he get for $5,700? How many $10 bills could he get for $5,700?

_____

_____

SUPER CHALLENGE: Fill in the chart by multiplying. What pattern do you see?

1 x 20	2 x 20	3 x 20	4 x 20	5 x 20
20				

6 x 20	7 x 20	8 x 20	9 x 20	10 x 20

Name: _____

THE WISE OLD PHILOSOPHER starring Woovis the Dog and Molly Mouse

FIGURE IT OUT!

1. Molly Mouse gives the Philosopher one dollar. How many 10¢ truths can she get for $1?_____

_____

2. Rudy Rabbit buys 2 truths, 2 wise thoughts, and 2 flashes of insight. How much does he spend?

_____

3. Moovis the Cow buys 2 truths, 2 wise thoughts, 2 flashes of insight, and 1 doughnut. She pays $1. How much change does she get back?

_____

4. Molly buys 4 truths, 6 wise thoughts, and 2 flashes of insight. How much does she spend?

_____

5. Rowena Pig spends exactly $1 on truth and doughnuts. She buys 1 truth. How many doughnuts does she buy?

_____

SUPER CHALLENGE: Think of one way to spend exactly one dollar on truths, wise thoughts, and doughnuts.

Name: _____

MAKIN' CHANGE starring Squirmy Worm and Judy Frog

FIGURE IT OUT!

1. If Squirmy Worm has one quarter, how many more quarters does he need to get one dollar?

_____

2. Squirmy has dimes and nickels that add up to 50¢. He has 6 coins in all. What coins does he have?

_____

3. Judy Frog has $1 in quarters and dimes. She has 5 dimes. How many quarters does she have?

_____

4. Woovis the Dog has $1 in quarters and nickels. He has 1 quarter. How many nickels does he have?

_____

5. Judy has pennies, nickels, and dimes that add up to $1. She has 5 nickels and 3 dimes. How many pennies does she have?

_____

SUPER CHALLENGE: Squirmy has quarters, dimes, and nickels that add up to $1.60. He has 4 dimes and 9 nickels. How many quarters does he have?

Comic-Strip Math: Problem-Solving © 2010 by Dan Greenberg, Scholastic Teaching Resources

Name: _____

DOGGY DINER starring Woovis the Dog and Rowena Pig

FIGURE IT OUT!

1. How much would 2 Trough Dinners cost?

_____

TROUGH MENU

TROUGH DINNER - $4.95
MUSH (CUP)------ $1.99
        (BOWL) --- $2.49
SCRAPS ---------- $1.25
SWILL ----------- $1.50
REGULAR SLOP--- $3.95
DELUXE SLOP----- $4.95

2. How much would a Trough Dinner and an order of Regular Slop cost?

_____

3. How much will a cup of Mush, one order of Scraps, and one order of Swill cost?

_____

4. Rowena has $15. Is that enough money to buy 3 Trough Dinners? Why or why not?

_____

5. Which costs more, 5 orders of Regular Slop or 4 orders of Deluxe Slop?

_____

6. Rowena's friend Purvis has $10 and wants 2 orders of Regular Slop and 1 Trough Dinner. How much more money does he need?

_____

SUPER CHALLENGE: How much money would Rowena need to buy 2 of everything on the menu?

Name: _____

TAKE IT TO THE BANK starring Judy Frog and Chuck Mantis

FIGURE IT OUT!

1. A guppy saves $10 each month and puts it in the bank. How much money does she have in the bank after 6 months?

_____

2. A trout has $80 in his checking account. He takes out $16 to buy a large bag of fish food. Then he deposits $64 the following week. How much money is in his account?

_____

3. A sea horse has $200 in her checking account. She deposits $35. Then she takes out $150 to buy a saddle the following week. How much money is left in her account?

_____

4. Chuck Mantis wants to put $270 in the bank. If he saves $9 a week, how many weeks will it take him to reach $270?

_____

5. The bank will give Judy Frog a free insect catcher if she puts $500 in the bank. She has $486. But she needs to spend $40 of that money to fix her lily pad. How much more money will she need to get the insect catcher?

_____

SUPER CHALLENGE: A codfish put $15 in the bank in January. Each month after that, she deposits twice as much as she did the month before. How many months will it take her to save more than $200?

Name: _____

LIVE AT THE HA-HA COMEDY CLUB starring Woovis the Dog

FIGURE IT OUT!

1. Woovis the Dog's Thursday comedy show sells 38 tickets for $4.00 each. How much money does the sale of the tickets bring in? _____

2. Woovis's Friday show sells 46 tickets for $4.75 each. How much money does the show take in?

_____

3. On Saturday morning, tickets cost $4.25. The Saturday morning show sells 50 tickets. How much money does the show take in?

_____

4. On Saturday afternoon, both $4.00 and $4.50 tickets are sold. In all, 22 tickets are sold for $4.00, and 28 tickets are sold for $4.50. How much money does the show take in?

_____

5. Which show took in more money—the Saturday morning show or the Saturday afternoon show? How much more?

_____

SUPER CHALLENGE: The Saturday night show has tickets for $4.50 and $5. Forty tickets for $4.50 are sold. In all, the show takes in a total of $300. How many $5 tickets are sold?

Name: _____

MOUSETRAP starring Woovis the Dog and Harry Horse

FIGURE IT OUT!

1. Woovis sells regular mousetraps for $4.95 each. How much will 3 regular mousetraps cost?

_____

2. How much will 12 regular mousetraps cost?

_____

3. Deluxe mousetraps cost $6.49 each. How much will 5 deluxe mousetraps cost?

_____

4. Which will cost more—6 regular mousetraps or 5 deluxe mousetraps? How much more?

_____

5. A customer has $150. What is the greatest number of regular mousetraps she can buy?

_____

SUPER CHALLENGE: A case of 24 regular mousetraps cost $99.95. How much money can Harry save by buying a case rather than buying the mousetraps separately?

Comic-Strip Math: Problem-Solving © 2010 by Dan Greenberg, Scholastic Teaching Resources

Name: _____

GO SKATING starring Woovis the Dog, Harry Horse, and Judy Frog

FIGURE IT OUT!

1. It costs 35 cents to rent 1 pair of skates. Woovis has 4 legs and needs 2 pairs of skates. How much will it cost him to rent 2 pairs of skates?_____

2. It costs $2.75 to skate at the rink. Woovis rents 2 pairs of skates. How much will it cost him to rent skates and skate at the rink?

_____

3. Woovis and Judy each rent 2 pairs of skates. What will be the total cost for both of them to rent skates and skate at the rink?

_____

4. Wendy Spider has 8 legs. She needs 4 pairs of skates. How much will it cost her to rent skates and skate at the rink?

_____

5. Squirmy Worm has 12 legs. Rudy the Red-Nosed Rabbit has 4 legs. How much will it cost the two of them to rent skates and go skating?

_____

SUPER CHALLENGE: How much would it cost a family of 16 rabbits to skate with rented skates? How much would they save if they brought their own skates?

Name: _____

MASTERPIECE starring Moovis the Cow and Squirmy Worm

FIGURE IT OUT!

1. Moovis the Cow sells her paintings for $9.95 each. How many paintings could Squirmy Worm buy for $20? Use estimation to find the answer.

_____

Use estimation to solve each problem.

2. How many $9.95 paintings could Squirmy buy for $50? For $80?

_____

3. Moovis sells her Deluxe paintings for $10.95 each. How many paintings could Squirmy buy for $100?

_____

4. Moovis has a new series of paintings called "Three Cows Sleeping in a Totally Dark Barn." Each painting sells for $6.02. Could someone buy 4 of these paintings with $20? Why or why not?

_____

5. How many $10 bills would Squirmy need to buy 3 paintings for $9.95?

_____

SUPER CHALLENGE: Woovis bought 10 paintings for $99.90. How much does each painting cost?

Name: _____

FOOD TO GO starring Woovis the Dog and Molly Mouse

Use estimation to solve each problem.

2. Molly Mouse gets Crumbs & Cheese for breakfast. She pays with the $5 bill. With the leftover money, what can Woovis buy to eat?

_____

3. Which item can Woovis buy with the $5 bill that will give the most change?

_____

4. Which two items can Woovis buy with the $5 bill so that he gets about $1 back in change?

_____

5. Woovis ordered two items from the menu and gave the cashier the $5 bill. But the two items cost more than $6.50. Which two items did Woovis order?

_____

SUPER CHALLENGE: Can Woovis use the $5 bill to buy three <u>different</u> items from the menu? Why or why not?

Name: _____

THE BIG DEAL starring Woovis the Dog and Wendy Spider

FIGURE IT OUT!

1. Rounded to the nearest hundred, how much would three $94 pencils cost?_____

Use estimation to solve each problem.

2. Wendy bought a notebook that costs $3.15 and stickers that cost $1.79. Is the total cost closer to $3.00, $5.00, or $10.00?

_____

3. Woovis went to the movies. A movie ticket cost $5.75. What was the cost of 1 movie ticket rounded to the nearest dollar?

_____

4. Woovis bought popcorn. The popcorn cost $3.19. What was the cost of the popcorn rounded to the nearest dollar?

_____

5. Woovis also bought a soda for $2.85. What was the total amount of money he spent at the movies rounded to the nearest dollar?

_____

SUPER CHALLENGE: Wendy bought a pair of jeans for $36.99, a hat for $8.65, and a coat for $52.49. What was the total cost of all 3 items rounded to the nearest dollar?

Name: _____

NEW JEANS starring Rowena Pig and Woovis the Dog

FIGURE IT OUT!

1. All jeans are on sale for $\frac{1}{4}$ off the regular price of $28. How much is $\frac{1}{4}$ of $28? _____

_____

2. How much would Rowena Pig pay for a pair of jeans on sale?

_____

3. Rowena wants to buy 2 pairs of jeans on sale. How much will she pay?

_____

4. In the Bonus Sale, you pay regular price for the first pair of jeans, then get $\frac{1}{2}$ off each additional pair. The regular price is $28. How much will Rowena pay for 2 pairs of jeans?

_____

5. Suppose Rowena decides to buy 3 pairs of jeans. How much will it cost to buy them for the sale price of $\frac{1}{4}$ off? How much will it cost to buy the 3 pairs using the Bonus Sale? Which sale would you choose?

_____

SUPER CHALLENGE:

The chart compares the regular, Sale, and Bonus Sale prices. Complete the chart.

	Regular Price	Sale Price	Bonus Sale Price
1 pair	$28		
2 pairs	$56		
3 pairs			
4 pairs			
5 pairs			

Name: _____

SPECIAL DELIVERY starring Ant Betty and Fangella the Snake

FIGURE IT OUT!

1. One gallon contains 4 quarts. How many quarts are there in 2 gallons of milk?

_____

2. How many quarts are there in 7 gallons of milk?

_____

3. Fangella had 20 quarts of milk. How many gallons does that equal?

_____

4. Fangella poured 10 quarts of milk into gallon containers. How many gallon containers did she fill? How many quarts were left over?

_____

5. There are 12 inches in 1 foot. How many inches long is a 4-foot snake?

_____

6. A group of ants formed a line 96 inches long. How long was the line in feet?

_____

SUPER CHALLENGE: The ants were carrying a string of foot-long hot dogs that was 54 inches long. How many whole feet was this? How many inches were left over?

Name: _____

STOP SIGN starring Rowena Pig and Woovis the Dog

FIGURE IT OUT!

1. Rowena Pig rides 25 yards on her bike to get from the first stop sign to the second one. How many feet apart are the stop signs? (One yard equals 3 feet.)_____

2. At the second stop sign, Rowena skids to a quick stop. Her bike leaves a 7-foot skid mark in the sand. How many inches long is the skid mark?

_____

Measurements
1 foot = 12 inches
1 yard = 3 feet
1 mile = 5,280 feet

3. Rowena rides 4 miles across town. How many feet does she ride?

_____

4. Rowena rides 30 feet. How many inches does she ride?

_____

5. Rowena rides 99 yards. How many feet does she ride?

_____

SUPER CHALLENGE: Rowena rides 40 yards. How many inches are there in 40 yards?

Name: _____

TRASH TALK starring Moovis the Cow and Molly Mouse

FIGURE IT OUT!

1. Moovis the Cow carries a 3-pound bag of garbage to the dump. One pound equals 16 ounces. How many ounces does the bag weigh?

_____

2. How many ounces are there in a 9-pound bag of garbage? A 22-pound bag of garbage?

_____

3. A bag weighs 64 ounces. How many pounds does it weigh?

_____

4. How many inches are there in a 14-foot-high pile of trash?

_____

5. How many feet are there in a 480-inch-high pile of trash?

_____

Measurements

1 pound = 16 ounces

1 foot = 12 inches

SUPER CHALLENGE: Measure the length of your classroom in feet. How long is your classroom in inches?

Name: _____

HIGHWAY ROBBERY starring Officer Woovis and Rowena Pig

FIGURE IT OUT!

1. Rowena Pig lives on the corner of 2nd Street and Avenue A. From her house she rides up Avenue A to 4th Street. How many blocks does she ride?_____

2. Rowena rides from the bank on 2nd Street and Avenue D to the bike shop on 5th Street and Avenue D. How many blocks does she ride?

_____

3. Rowena rides up Avenue A from her house to the park on 5th Street and Avenue E. How many blocks does she ride?

_____

4. Rowena rides up 4th Street from Avenue B to Avenue E. Then she turns around and rides back to Avenue A. How many blocks does she ride?

_____

5. Rowena goes for a bike ride. She starts at 3rd Street and Avenue E. She rides to 3rd Street and Avenue B. Then she turns right to 2nd Street and Avenue B. How many blocks does she ride?

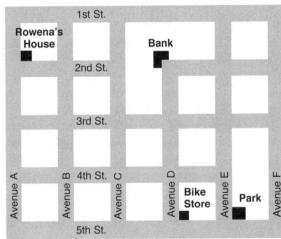

SUPER CHALLENGE: Rowena can go from her house to the bank by riding up 1st Street or by riding up 3rd street. Which way is shorter?

Name: _____

THE TEXAN starring Rowena Pig and Squirmy Worm

FIGURE IT OUT!

1. Squirmy wants to travel from El Paso to Lubbock. How many miles are between the 2 cities. Use the map below to answer the question.

_____

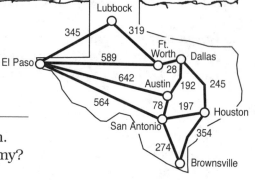

2. After going from El Paso to Lubbock, Squirmy went to Forth Worth. How many miles did he travel in all?

_____

3. Rowena traveled straight from El Paso to Forth Worth. How many fewer miles did Rowena travel than Squirmy?

_____

4. How many miles would a round-trip between Houston and Brownsville cover?

_____

5. Which route from San Antonio to Lubbock covers 789 miles?

_____

6. Which is the shortest route from San Antonio to Lubbock?

_____

SUPER CHALLENGE: Find a route that goes through every city on the map. Write it down on a separate sheet of paper. How many miles is your route?

Name: _____

ROUND TRIP starring Woovis the Dog and Harry Horse

2. How long is a trip from the Old Travel Agency to the Old Tree, to the Old Barn, and back to the Old Travel Agency?

_____

3. How long is a trip from the Old Travel Agency, to the Old Tree, to the Old Barn, back to the Old Tree, to the Old Mill, back to the Old Tree, then back to the Old Travel Agency?

_____

4. What is the shortest trip that begins at the Old Travel Agency and ends at the Old Pond?

_____

5. Which route from the Old Travel Agency to the Old Pond covers 9 miles?

_____

SUPER CHALLENGE: Woovis went from the Old Travel Agency to the Old Tree. Then he went to one other place before coming back to the Old Travel Agency. He went 13 miles in all. Where did Woovis go?

Name: _____

WHAT'S HOPPIN' AGAIN starring Judy Frog and Rudy Rabbit

FIGURE IT OUT!

1. Look at the graph below. Starting at square X, Judy hopped 4 squares up and 3 squares to the right. In which square did she land?

_____

NOTE: Judy and Rudy can hop in vertical and horizontal directions only.

2. Rudy is in square X. Which are the 2 shortest paths he can take to get to square E?

_____

3. Judy is in square A. Which are the 2 shortest paths she can take to get to square E?

_____

4. Find the 2 shortest paths to get from square X to square D.

_____

5. Starting at square X, Rudy hopped 6 squares up and 5 squares to the left. How many squares is he from square D?

_____

SUPER CHALLENGE: Find 3 paths to get from square D to square E. Does each path contain the same total number of squares?

Name: _____

DOCTOR KNOWS BEST AGAIN starring Dr. Woovis and Rudy Rabbit

FIGURE IT OUT!

1. After his paw healed, Rudy practiced the piano. The graph below shows his practice record. On which day did he practice the longest? _____

2. On which day or days did Rudy practice less than 5 minutes?

_____

3. On which day or days did Rudy practice more than 45 minutes?

_____

4. Did Rudy practice more on Day 3 than he did on Day 6?

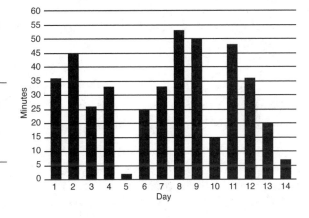

_____

5. On which days did Rudy practice the same amount of time?

_____

6. Was Rudy's combined practice time for Days 6 and 10 more or less than his practice time on Day 2?

_____

SUPER CHALLENGE: On Day 15, Rudy practiced for half the time that he practiced on Day 9. How long did he practice on Day 15?

Name: _____

MAGIC SHOW starring Woovis the Dog and Ant Betty

FIGURE IT OUT!

1. Woovis smashed several pumpkins. The graph below shows the results. How many pieces did the 10-pound pumpkin smash into?

_____

2. How many pieces did the 30-pound pumpkin smash into?

_____

3. How many more pieces did the 40-pound pumpkin smash into than the 30-pound pumpkin?

_____

4. How many 10-pound pumpkins do you need to smash to get the same number of pieces in a 40-pound smashed pumpkin?

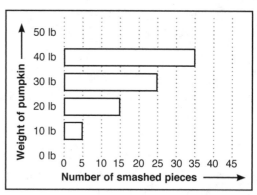

_____

5. Look at the pattern on the graph. How many pieces would you expect a 50-pound pumpkin to smash into? Draw a bar on the graph.

_____

SUPER CHALLENGE: How many pieces would you expect a 100-pound pumpkin to smash into?

Comic-Strip Math: Problem-Solving © 2010 by Dan Greenberg, Scholastic Teaching Resources

Name: _____

WEATHERMAN starring Woovis the Dog and Rudy Rabbit

FIGURE IT OUT!

1. Showers on Monday morning produced 0.5 inches of rain by noon. By 6 p.m., a total of 2 inches of rain had fallen. How many inches of rain fell between noon and 6 p.m.?_____

2. On Tuesday, 1.2 inches of rain fell. Two more inches of rain fell the next day. How many inches of rain fell on Wednesday?

_____

3. The graph shows the high temperatures for Wednesday through Sunday. On which day was the highest temperature reached? The lowest? What was the difference between the two temperatures?

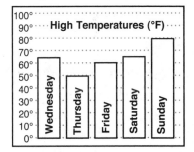

_____

4. Between which two days did the temperature drop 15 degrees? Increase by 15 degrees?

_____

5. Saturday's low temperature was 38°. How many degrees did the temperature rise to reach Saturday's high temperature?

_____

SUPER CHALLENGE: What was the average high temperature for all five days shown on the graph?

Name: _____

NEW JOB starring Ant Betty and Judy Frog

FIGURE IT OUT!

1. What does each ⬤ stand for in the pictograph?

_____

JUDY'S HOURS

MONDAY
Start Time: 12 PM

TUESDAY
Start Time: 10:30 AM

WEDNESDAY
Start Time: 9:15 AM

KEY

⬤ = 1 HOUR   ◗ = $\frac{1}{2}$ HOUR

◔ = $\frac{3}{4}$ HOUR   ◗ = $\frac{1}{4}$ HOUR

2. How many hours did Judy work on Monday? Tuesday?

_____

3. How many more hours did Judy work on Tuesday than on Monday?

_____

4. On Thursday, Judy worked 7 hours and 15 minutes. Draw what that would look like on the pictograph.

5. On Friday, Judy worked 4 hours and 45 minutes more than she did on Monday. How many hours did Judy work on Friday? Draw your answer in pictograph form.

SUPER CHALLENGE: How many hours did Judy work on Monday, Tuesday, and Wednesday? Draw your answer in pictograph form.

72

Comic-Strip Math: Problem-Solving © 2010 by Dan Greenberg, Scholastic Teaching Resources

Name: _____

A BEAR IN FULL starring Monica Bear and Ant Betty

FIGURE IT OUT!

1. Monica Bear's new mirror measures 72 inches by 60 inches. What is the perimeter of the mirror?

_____

2. Another mirror is shaped like a square. That means that all 4 sides are the same length. The mirror's perimeter is 24 inches. How long is each side?

_____

3. Ant Betty's full-length mirror is $3\frac{1}{2}$ inches across and $4\frac{1}{2}$ inches down. What is its perimeter?

_____

4. Which has a greater perimeter, a mirror that measures $8\frac{1}{2}$ inches across and 12 inches down or a mirror that measures $12\frac{1}{2}$ inches across and 8 inches down?

_____

5. Mirror A measures 5 inches across and 7 inches down. Mirror B measures 8 inches across and 3 inches down. Which mirror's perimeter is bigger? How much bigger?

_____

SUPER CHALLENGE: A mirror is shaped like a rectangle. Its width is twice as long as its height. The mirror is 11 inches high. What is its width? What is the mirror's perimeter?

Name: _____

FUN BOX starring Ant Betty and Fangella the Snake

FIGURE IT OUT!

1. Each square side of the box is 8 inches long. What is the perimeter of 1 square side?_____

2. Each square side of another box is 18 inches long. What is the perimeter of one square side?

_____

3. Each side of a square is 3.25 inches long. What is the square's perimeter?

_____

4. The length of a rectangle is 12 feet. The width of the rectangle is 8 feet. What is the rectangle's perimeter?

_____

5. Another rectangle has a length of 8.25 inches and a width of 5.5 inches. What is the rectangle's perimeter?

_____

6. A hexagon has 6 sides that each measure 2.4 inches. What is the hexagon's perimeter?

_____

SUPER CHALLENGE: A pentagon has a perimeter of 62 inches. Its 5 sides are all the same length. What is the length of each side?

Comic-Strip Math: Problem-Solving © 2010 by Dan Greenberg, Scholastic Teaching Resources

Name: _____

MONEY BACK starring Woovis the Dog and Sal and Al Gator

FIGURE IT OUT!

1. Sal and Al plant their bird seeds in a square garden that measures 6 feet on each of its 4 sides. What is the perimeter of their garden?

   _____

2. What is the area of Sal and Al's bird seed garden in square feet?

   _____

3. Al's flower garden is a rectangle that is 8 yards long and 3 yards wide. What is the garden's perimeter?

   _____

4. One yard equals 3 feet. What is the perimeter of Al's garden in feet?

   _____

5. What is the area of Al's garden in square yards?

   _____

6. What is the length and width of Al's garden in feet?

   _____

7. What is the area of Al's garden in square feet?

   _____

SUPER CHALLENGE: Woovis has his own garden that is shaped like a rectangle. It has a width of 5 yards and an area of 55 square yards. What is the garden's length? What is the perimeter of Woovis's garden in feet?

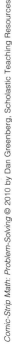

Name: _____

THE HAMMER starring Woovis the Dog and Rudy Rabbit

FIGURE IT OUT!

1. Rudy Rabbit pounds 3 nails into a piece of wood. The nails are not in a straight line. What shape will he get if he draws lines to connect the nails?_____

2. Rudy pounds 4 nails to form 4 right angles. The nails are all 3 inches apart. What shape does Rudy make? Draw the shape.

_____

3. Woovis the Dog attaches a pencil to a nail with a string. Then he pulls the string tight and swings it around. What shape does the pencil draw?

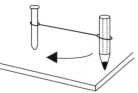

_____

4. Moovis the Cow pounds 4 nails to form 4 right angles. Two nails are 3 inches apart. Two other nails are 4 inches apart. What shape does Moovis make? Draw the shape.

_____

5. Each side of a triangle is 10 inches long. What is the distance around the triangle?

_____

SUPER CHALLENGE: Here are some true statements about a square: It has 4 sides. It has right angles. Write one other true statement about a square.

Name: _____

PIE AND PI starring Woovis the Dog and Moovis the Cow

THE MOOVIS AND WOOVIS SHOW

I'm Woovis.

I'm Moovis.

Hey Woovis, which is the left side of this blueberry pie?

That's easy. It's the part you haven't eaten yet.

FIGURE IT OUT!

1. The pie pan has a radius (r) of 6 inches. This is the distance from the center to the outside edge. Use the formula $C = 2 \times \pi \times r$ to find the circumference (C). This is the distance around the outside of the pan. The number π equals 3.14. _____

2. What is the circumference around a pie with a radius of 12 inches?

_____

3. The diameter (d) is the distance all the way across a circle. If the diameter is 4 feet, what is the circumference of the circle?

_____

4. Use the formula $A = \pi r^2$ to find the area of a pie with a 6-inch radius in square inches.

_____

5. What is the area of a pie with a 3.5 meter radius?

_____

SUPER CHALLENGE: Calculate the circumference of the circle. What is the distance around the outside of the shaded half of the circle? What is the area of the shaded half of the circle?

d = 20 in

Name: _____

LUCKY SEVEN starring Rudy Rabbit and Monica Bear

FIGURE IT OUT!

1. What number is missing from this number pattern?

5, 11, 17, 23, 29, ___, 41, 47

2. The underlined number in this pattern is wrong. What number should go in its place? 4, 12, 20, 28, 36, <u>42</u>, 52

_____

3. Replace the underlined number in this pattern with the correct number.
2, 4, 8, 16, <u>24</u>, 64, 128

_____

4. Write the next three letters in this pattern: A, C, E, G, I, __, __, __.

_____

5. Write the next three numbers in this pattern: 407, 396, 385, 374, 363, __, __, __.

_____

SUPER CHALLENGE: Find the wrong number in this pattern. Then write the number that should go in its place: 1, 3, 9, 27, 36, 243

ROOF ROOF starring Woovis the Dog, Chuck Mantis, and Judy Frog

FIGURE IT OUT!

1. Section A (below) at Ha Ha's has 3 rows with 3 seats in each row. In how many seats would you have a neighbor on both your left side and your right side?_____

2. In how many seats in Section A would you have a neighbor on only one side?

_____

Section A

3. Section B has 3 rows with 4 seats in each row. In how many seats would you have a neighbor on both your left side and your right side?

_____

Section B

4. In how many seats in Section A would you have a neighbor on all 4 sides—on your left, on your right, in front of you, and behind you?

_____

Section C

5. In how many seats in Section B would you have a neighbor on all 4 sides?

_____

SUPER CHALLENGE: Section C has 3 rows with 5 seats in each row. In how many seats in Section C would you have a neighbor on all 4 sides? In how many seats would you have a neighbor on both your left side and your right side?

Name: _____

SNOOZER starring Woovis the Dog and Moovis the Cow

FIGURE IT OUT!

1. Moovis snores 720 times in 1 hour. How many times does she snore in half an hour?

_____

Hint: There are 60 minutes in an hour.

2. How many times does Moovis snore in 15 minutes?
How many times does she snore in 1 minute?

_____

3. Harry the Horse snores 660 times in 1 hour.
How many times does he snore in 1 minute?

_____

4. In 2 hours, how many more times will Moovis snore than Harry?

_____

5. Steve the Hummingbird snores 84 times in 6 minutes. How many times does he snore in 1 hour?

_____

SUPER CHALLENGE: Ant Betty snores 1.5 times faster than Steve. How many times does Ant Betty snore in 1 hour? How many times does Ant Betty snore in 20 minutes? How many times does she snore in 3 minutes?

Name: _____

PULSATIONS starring Dr. Woovis and Rudy Rabbit

2. How many times will Rudy's heart beat in 10 minutes? How many times will it beat in 30 minutes? How many times will it beat in 1 hour?

_____

3. Woovis measures Harry the Horse's heartbeat. In 30 seconds, Harry's heart beats 38 times. How many times will his heart beat in 1 minute?

_____

4. Does Harry's heart beat faster or slower than Rudy's heart? By how much does Harry's heart beat faster or slower?

_____

5. There are 60 seconds in 1 minute. Judy the Frog's heart beats 20 times in 15 seconds. How many times does her heart beat in 1 minute? How many times will it beat in half an hour?

_____

SUPER CHALLENGE: Woovis's heart beats 5,400 times in 1 hour. How many times does it beat in 1 day? How many times does it beat in 3 days? How many times does it beat in 1 week?

Name: _____

HUMS starring Harry Horse and Steve Hummingbird

2. How many times will Steve's wings beat in 5 seconds?

_____

3. Steve's friend Molly beats her wings 28 times in each second. How many times will Molly's wings beat in 13 seconds?

_____

4. Steve's wings beat 200 times. How long did it take the wings to beat?

_____

5. There are 60 seconds in 1 minute. How many times will Steve's wings beat in 2 minutes?

_____

6. How many seconds will it take Steve to beat his wings 1,000 times? How many seconds will it take for Molly's wings to beat 2,100 times?

_____

SUPER CHALLENGE: In one hour, how many more times will Molly's wings beat than Steve's wings?

Comic-Strip Math: Problem-Solving © 2010 by Dan Greenberg, Scholastic Teaching Resources

Name: _____

NONTOXIC starring Squirmy Worm and Fangella the Snake

FIGURE IT OUT!

1. Fangella sticks out her tongue once every 4 seconds. There are 60 seconds in 1 minute. How many times will she stick it out in 1 minute? _____

2. How many times will Fangella stick out her tongue in 3 minutes?

_____

3. How many times will Fangella stick out her tongue in half an hour (or 30 minutes)?

_____

4. Fangella is 48 inches long. Squirmy is 4 inches long. How many times longer is Fangella than Squirmy?

_____

5. Fangella traveled 60 miles to the Snake Convention. It took her 4 days to get there and she traveled the same number of miles each day. How many miles did she travel each day?

_____

SUPER CHALLENGE: Fangella belonged to the Mini-Viper snake group. For a period of 4 days, she collected $12 from all 43 members of the group for T-shirts. How much did Fangella collect in total? How much money did she average per day?

Name: _____

SPEED TRAP starring Officer Woovis and Rowena Pig

FIGURE IT OUT!

1. A car traveled 36 miles per hour (mph) in a 15 mph speed zone. How much over the speed limit was the car traveling?

_____

2. Rowena was driving a car 21 miles over the 25 mph speed limit. How fast was she going?

_____

3. Yesterday, Rowena went 29 mph in a 40 mph speed zone. How far under the speed limit was she traveling?

_____

4. Harry the Horse's car traveled 35 miles in each hour. How many miles did Harry drive his car in 5 hours?

_____

5. Rowena's car traveled 17 miles in each hour. How many miles did she drive her car in 12 hours?

_____

SUPER CHALLENGE: Rowena drove her car 3 times. The first trip was 7 miles, the second trip was 22 miles, and the third trip was 13 miles. What was the average driving distance for the 3 trips?

Name: _____

FAMILY REUNION PICNIC starring Woovis the Dog and Rowena Pig

FIGURE IT OUT!

1. What was the ratio of grandparents to uncles at the picnic? Write your answer in simplest form.

_____

Write all ratios in simplest form.

2. What was the ratio of uncles to cousins at the picnic?

_____

3. Eight of the cousins at the picnic were boys. How many of the cousins were girls? What was the ratio of girl cousins to boy cousins?

_____

4. What was the ratio of boy cousins to all cousins at the picnic?

_____

5. What was the ratio of girl cousins to uncles at the picnic?

_____

6. What was the ratio of grandparents to cousins and uncles?

_____

7. What was the ratio of ants to all others at the picnic?

_____

SUPER CHALLENGE: Seventy percent or 70 out of every 100 ants at the picnic were hungry. How many of the ants were not hungry?

Name: _____

TALENTED TONGUE starring Harry Horse and Judy Frog

FIGURE IT OUT!

1. Using RIBBIT and CROAK, a frog can make these 2-word phrases: RIBBIT-CROAK and CROAK-RIBBIT. What 2-word phrases can a dog make of BARK and RUFF? (Use each word only once in each phrase.)_____

2. How many different 2-word phrases can a dog make out of the words BARK and GRR? Write each arrangement.

_____

3. How many different 2-word phrases can a dog make out of the words BARK, GRR, and RUFF? Write each arrangement.

_____

4. How many different 2-word phrases can a cat make out of the words MEOW, PURR, and SSS? Write each arrangement.

_____

5. How many different 3-word phrases can a cat make out of the words MEOW, PURR, and SSS? Write each arrangement.

_____

SUPER CHALLENGE: How many different 3-word phrases could a cat make out of the words MEOW, PURR, and SSS if each phrase must start with the word PURR?

Name: _____

MATH WHIZ starring Squirmy Worm, Ant Betty, and Itchy Squirrel

FIGURE IT OUT!

1. Itchy Squirrel scores 86, 73, 47, 93, and 81 on her math tests. What is her high score? What is her low score? _____

2. The range of Itchy's scores is the difference between her high and low scores. What is her range?

_____

3. Arrange Itchy's scores in problem 1 from lowest to highest. The median is the middle score in the group. What is her median score?

_____

4. The mean score is the average score. To find the mean, add all the scores. Then divide the total by the number of scores. What is the mean of Itchy's scores in problem 1?

_____

5. The mode is the score that appears the most in a group. Find the mode from this group of quiz scores: 16, 15, 18, 20, 15, 13, 15, 13, 19.

SUPER CHALLENGE: Roll a number cube 25 times. Record the scores. Find the range, mean, median, and mode of your scores.

ANSWERS

Page 8
1. Six thousand, seven hundred, eighty-nine
2. The digit 8 occupies the tens' place.
3. The digit 9 is in the ones' place.
4. Four hundred, seventy-six thousand, seven hundred, eighty-nine
5. The digit 4 is in the hundred thousands' place.
6. The digit 7 occupies the ten thousands' place and the hundreds' place.
Super Challenge: 12,500,00; 12,000,000.

Page 9
1. 20 years
2. 50 years
3. 130 years; 100 years
4. 500 years; 450 years
5. 700 years; 1,000 years
Super Challenge: 950

Page 10
1. 70 feet
2. 50 feet
3. 57 feet
4. 45 feet
5. 71 feet
Super Challenge: 110 feet

Page 11
1. They told 11 jokes in all.
2. The audience laughed at 9 jokes.
3. They were on stage for 24 minutes after the intermission.
4. The show played for 15 nights in all.
5. Woovis earned $6 for each show. Moovis earned $4 for each show.
Super Challenge: Answers will vary.

Page 12
1. 20 buttons
2. 56 buttons
3. 30 mice
4. 126 buttons
5. 8 buttons
Super Challenge: 6 teams

Page 13
1. 20 pills
2. 3 small bottles
3. 14 days
4. 49 days
5. 126 pills
Super Challenge: 252 pills

Page 14
1. Four rabbits have 16 feet.
2. There are 6 rabbits in the group.
3. Twenty legs were doing cartwheels.
4. They bought 132 sneakers.
5. There are 9 animals walking.
6. Fifty legs are walking in all.
Super Challenge: Answers will vary.

Page 15
1. He takes 40 steps.
2. She takes 9 steps with each of her 8 legs.
3. Susan takes 40 more steps than Sharon.
4. He takes 240 steps in all.
5. She takes 49 steps with her other legs.
Super Challenge: No. Gary takes 156 steps. The spiders took 224 steps.

Page 16
1. She climbed 18 steps.
2. She climbed 45 steps.
3. He ended up on the 5th floor.
4. He walked up 54 steps.
5. He descended 72 steps.
6. She ended up on the 5th floor.
Super Challenge: The new answer would be 35 steps.

Page 17
1. Eight cows were in each tree.
2. There were 16 animals in each tree.
3. There were 6 trees in all.
4. There were 35 cows in all.
5. Six cows hid in each tree.
Super Challenge: Sixteen cows jumped over the fence each minute.

Page 18

1. Each player will win $12,500.
2. Each player will win $6,250.
3. There would be 20 players.
4. The winner won $50,000. The other two players each won $25,000.
5. The 4th place finisher won $4,000.

Super Challenge: Answers will vary. Check to see that each successive finisher receives twice as much prize money as the next lowest finisher.

Page 19

1. He could make 4 pots of soup with 2 carrots left over.
2. He needs 168 carrots to make the soup. He needs 112 carrots to make the soup.
3. He can make 9 pots of soup. He can make 18 pots of soup.
4. He can make 14 pots of soup with 2 carrots left over.
5. He can make 9 pots of 7-carrot soup. He can make 4 pots of 14-carrot soup. The 14-carrot soup will have 7 carrrots left over.

Super Challenge: Rudy can make twice as many pots of 7-carrot soup as 14-carrot soup no matter how many carrots he begins with.

Page 20

1. 6 feet
2. 18 feet
3. 96 points
4. 450 points
5. 8 two-point baskets

Super Challenge: 90 points

Page 21

1. 29
2. 10
3. 22
4. 60
5. Answers will vary.

Super Challenge: Answers will vary, but none of the products should be higher than 100. (The highest possible answer is 93.)

Page 22

1. 60 brothers
2. 80 pebbles
3. 30 sisters
4. 81 minutes
5. 581 worms

Super Challenge: More than half want to become lawyers.

Page 23

1. Tiger has 21 teeth now.
2. Tiger Smith has 35 stripes.
3. Yes. Tiger Brown has 32 stripes.
4. She saw 6 patients yesterday.
5. There are 4 spiders in the group.

Super Challenge: Tiger Jones played for 16 hours on Sunday and for 4 hours on Friday. He played 12 hours longer on Sunday than he did on Friday.

Page 24

1. The President serves 12 years.
2. He served 4 terms.
3. She served 6 terms.
4. A total of 251 members have to vote to pass a law.
5. The law got 262 votes.

Super Challenge: 350 must vote to make change.

Page 25

1. 12 stalls
2. 12 bales
3. 4 bales
4. $\frac{1}{4}$ of the chickens
5. 24 pigs

Super Challenge: $\frac{3}{10}$ of the horses

Page 26

1. $\frac{1}{2}$ white, $\frac{1}{2}$ black
2. $\frac{4}{7}$ black, $\frac{3}{7}$ white
3. $\frac{1}{4}$ black
4. 2 red socks, 4 green socks
5. $\frac{2}{5}$ red

Super Challenge: 5 yellow socks, 7 red and white socks

Page 27
1. $\frac{1}{4}$
2. $\frac{1}{2}$
3. $\frac{2}{3}$
4. 9 feet
5. 2 feet
Super Challenge: You would need to climb 7 feet to get halfway up Fred's neck. To get halfway up Ed's neck, you would need to climb 6 feet. The distance halfway up Fred's neck is greater than the distance halfway up Ed's neck by 1 foot.

Page 28
1. $10\frac{4}{5}$ minutes
2. $2\frac{5}{6}$ minutes
3. $5\frac{1}{2}$ minutes
4. $11\frac{3}{8}$ minutes
5. $57\frac{1}{2}$ minutes
Super Challenge: $23\frac{3}{4}$ minutes

Page 29
1. $8\frac{1}{4}$ inches
2. $7\frac{1}{3}$ ounces
3. $2\frac{1}{4}$ ounces
4. $1\frac{2}{3}$ ounces
5. The $2\frac{1}{4}$-ounce snowballs weigh more. They weigh $\frac{7}{12}$ of an ounce more.
Super Challenge: blue cup

Page 30
1. 30¢
2. 1 mile; 50¢
3. Woovis drove the skunk $\frac{1}{10}$ of a mile farther.
4. $\frac{7}{8}$ of a mile
5. $\frac{7}{10}$ of a mile
Super Challenge: $\frac{13}{18}$ of a mile

Page 31
1. $\frac{1}{2}$
2. $\frac{3}{4}$ of the baseballs were caught.
3. Judy caught 6 flies.
4. Judy caught $\frac{1}{3}$ of the groundballs.
5. Judy caught $\frac{1}{3}$ of the insects.
Super Challenge: Woovis did not get a hit $\frac{7}{10}$ of the time.

Page 32
1. $\frac{2}{3}$ of the cocoa was left.
2. He drank $\frac{2}{3}$ of the mug.
3. $\frac{1}{2}$ of the mug was filled with cocoa.
4. $\frac{1}{3}$ of the tea was left in the mug.
5. You need to add $\frac{1}{3}$ of a full glass.
Super Challenge: You can add 6 ladles. $\frac{1}{4}$ of a cup will be left over.

Page 33
1. Sal grew $3\frac{1}{4}$ inches in the two months.
2. Sal grew $\frac{1}{2}$ inch more.
3. Sal grew a total of 5 inches.
4. Sal grew $\frac{3}{4}$ inch more.
5. Sal grew a total of $2\frac{1}{8}$ inches.
6. Sal grew $1\frac{3}{8}$ inches more.
Super Challenge: Answers will vary.

Page 34
1. It rained 1 inch.
2. It rained $\frac{1}{4}$ inch more on the first day than on the second day.
3. The two threads are $7\frac{1}{4}$ inches long.
4. Uncle Walter is $1\frac{7}{8}$ inches longer than Squirmy.
5. Squirmy will be $2\frac{19}{24}$ inches long.
Super Challenge: Answers will vary.

Page 35
1. Woovis danced with 18 dogs.
2. Rowena danced with 16 pigs.
3. Woovis danced with 2 more partners.
4. Eight partners were not clumsy.
5. Woovis and Rowena danced with $\frac{17}{22}$ of the dance partners.
Super Challenge: Four different couples can be formed: Woovis and Rowena; Woovis and Fangella; Harry and Rowena; Harry and Fangella.

Page 36
1. Rudy climbed $\frac{1}{2}$ of the way to the top.
2. Rudy needs to climb to the 25th floor.
3. The 20th floor is $\frac{1}{5}$ of the way to the top.
4. Rudy needs to climb to the 40th floor.
5. Rudy needs to climb 7 floors.
6. The 30th floor is less than $\frac{1}{3}$ of the way up the building. $\frac{1}{3}$ of the way up the building is approximately the 33rd floor.

Super Challenge: Being on the 60th floor of an 80-story building would be higher. Being on the 60th floor of an 80-story is $\frac{3}{4}$ the way up the building. Being on the 60th floor of a 100-story building is $\frac{3}{5}$ the way up the building. $\frac{3}{4}$ is greater than $\frac{3}{5}$.

Page 37
1. $\frac{5}{12}$ of the snakes order soup.
2. $\frac{7}{12}$ of the snakes did not order soup.
3. $\frac{1}{2}$ of the rabbits ordered cake.
4. Three pigs order slop.
5. $\frac{2}{3}$ of the pigs did not order slop.
Super Challenge: Thirteen snakes and rabbits order ice cream.

Page 38
1. 2.3 feet
2. 3.5 feet
3. 0.5 foot
4. 2.8 feet
5. 5.6 feet high
Super Challenge: Ed's boots should be 7.8 feet tall. Fred's boots should be 5.5 feet tall. Jed's boots should be 13.4 feet tall.

Page 39
1. 1.2 meters
2. 6.4 meters
3. 20 steps
4. 20 meters
5. 25 meters is higher by 1 meter
Super Challenge: 250 steps

Page 40
1. 8.6 pounds
2. 10 sandwiches
3. The 0.8-pound tuna sandwich weighs 0.54 pounds more.
4. Each lunch bag will weigh 0.98 pounds. The total weight of the lunch bags is 8.82 pounds.
5. Two 2.2-pound lunches and one 1.6-pound lunch
Super Challenge: Three 1.6-pound lunches (4.8 pounds); two 1.6-pound lunches and one 2.5-pound lunch (5.7 pounds); two 1.6-pound lunches and one 2.2-pound lunch (5.4 pounds)

Page 41
1. 1.15 minutes
2. 5.4 minutes
3. 11.4 minutes
4. 8 bolt locks
5. 8 key locks
Super Challenge: 32 bolt locks

Page 42
1. 448.4 pounds
2. 271.2 pounds
3. 177.2 pounds
4. 11 times heavier
5. 119 times heavier
Super Challenge: Yes. Monica weighs about 10.8 times more than Woovis.

Page 43
1. The hour hand will be at 12 and the minute hand at 6; 6 will be covered.
2. 1:05
3. 2:00, 2:30, 3:00, 3:30, 4:00, 4:30
4. 3:30
5. 12:00, 12:12, 12:24, 12:36, 12:48, 1:00, 1:12, 1:24, 1:36, 1:48, 2:00
Super Challenge: 22 times

Page 44
1. 11:45
2. 9:00
3. 5:25; 5:53
4. 12:05; 12:45
5. 6:51; 12:00
Super Challenge: 2:58; 2:26

Page 45
1. Judy slept for 10 hours in all.
2. That is $9\frac{1}{2}$ hours of sleep.
3. She should wake up at 8 a.m.
4. Al Gator slept for 9 hours.
5. He slept for 11 hours.
Super Challenge: Judy should set her alarm for 7:30 a.m.

Page 46
1. The cake was in the oven for 1 hour and 45 minutes before it began burning.
2. The cake will begin burning at 2:10 p.m.
3. The pie was done at 10:50 a.m.
4. The pie will be done at 1:00 p.m.
5. She finished work at 5:15 p.m.
Super Challenge: Answers will vary.

Page 47

1. The movie will end at 12:45 p.m.
2. The second show begins at 1 p.m.
3. The third show began at 2:45 p.m. No, he will not arrive on time.
4. Yes. He can go to the 6:15 p.m. show that ends at 7:45 p.m.
5. Twice. The movie is shown at the beginning of the hour at 1 p.m. and 8 p.m.

Super Challenge: The movie will be shown at 4 p.m.

Page 48

1. It will take her about 5 hours to finish the book.
2. It will take him about 7 hours to finish the book.
3. He can read about 348 pages in 6 hours.
4. It will take about 9 hours for Woovis to read the book.
5. It will take Moovis about 10 to 11 hours to read the book.

Super Challenge: She can buy *Moo Over Miami* and *The Big Moo* for under $5. She can buy *Moo Over Miami* and *Cow for a Day* for under $6. She can buy *Cow for a Day* and *The Moo Lagoon* for under $10.

Page 49

1. January 31
2. January 14 and January 17
3. Friday
4. February 1
5. 28 days

Super Challenge: January 22

Page 50

1. $20
2. $40; $60; $100
3. $800; $1,600; $2,500
4. 4 $100 bills; 40 $10 bills
5. 57 $100 bills; 570 $10 bills

Super Challenge:

1 x 20	2 x 20	3 x 20	4 x 20	5 x 20
20	40	60	80	100

6 x 20	7 x 20	8 x 20	9 x 20	10 x 20
120	140	160	180	200

Each answer is 20 greater than the previous answer.

Page 51

1. 10 truths
2. 74¢
3. 8¢
4. $1.42
5. 5 doughnuts

Super Challenge: 7 truths, 1 wise thought, 1 doughnut OR 1 truth, 3 wise thoughts, 3 doughnuts OR 4 truths, 2 wise thoughts, 2 doughnuts

Page 52

1. 3 quarters
2. 4 dimes and 2 nickels
3. 2 quarters
4. 15 nickels
5. 45 pennies

Super Challenge: 3 quarters

Page 53

1. Two Trough Dinners would cost $9.90.
2. A Trough Dinner and an order of Regular Slop would cost $8.90.
3. A cup of Mush, one order of Scraps, and one order of Swill would cost $4.74.
4. Fifteen dollars is enough money. You know because $4.95 is less than $5.00. Three times $4.95 must be less than 3 times $5, or $15.
5. Four orders of Deluxe Slop cost 5 cents more.
6. Purvis needs $2.85 more.

Super Challenge: She would need $42.16.

Page 54

1. $60
2. $128
3. $85
4. 30 weeks
5. $54

Super Challenge: 4 months

Page 55

1. $152
2. $218.50
3. $212.50
4. $214
5. The Saturday afternoon show took in $1.50 more.

Super Challenge: Twenty-four $5 tickets were sold.

Page 56

1. Three regular mousetraps will cost $14.85.
2. Twelve regular mousetraps will cost $59.40.
3. Five deluxe mousetraps will cost $32.45.
4. Five deluxe mousetraps cost $2.75 more than 6 regular mousetraps.
5. She can buy 30 mousetraps.

Super Challenge: Harry can save $18.85.

Page 57

1. It will cost 70 cents to rent 2 pairs of skates.
2. It will cost $3.45 to rent skates and skate.
3. The total cost will be $6.90.
4. The cost will be $4.15.
5. It will cost $8.30 to rent skates and go skating.

Super Challenge: It will cost $55.20 to rent skates and skate. They would save $11.20 if they brought their own skates.

Page 58

1. 2 paintings
2. 5 paintings for $50; 8 paintings for $80
3. 9 paintings
4. No. Four paintings cost more than $24.
5. 3 $10 bills

Super Challenge: $9.99

Page 59

1. Deluxe Scraps
2. Kibble or Mouse Crumbs
3. Mouse Crumbs
4. Table Scraps and Mouse Crumbs
5. Crumbs & Cheese and Deluxe Scraps

Super Challenge: Woovis can't buy three different items with $5. The cheapest three items cost a combined $5.67.

Page 60

1. They would cost $300.00.
2. The cost of the stickers and notebook is closer to $5.00.
3. The cost of 1 movie ticket rounded to the nearest dollar was $6.00.
4. The cost of the popcorn rounded to the nearest dollar was $3.00.
5. The total amount of money spent rounded to the nearest dollar is $12.00.

Super Challenge: The total cost of the 3 items rounded to the nearest dollar was $98.00.

Page 61

1. $7
2. $21
3. $42
4. $42
5. It costs $63 to buy 3 pairs of jeans at the sale price of $\frac{1}{4}$ off. With the Bonus Sale, it costs $56 to buy 3 pairs of jeans. The Bonus Sale is a better deal.

Super Challenge:

	Regular Price	Sale Price	Bonus Sale Price
1 pair	$28	$21	$28
2 pairs	$56	$42	$42
3 pairs	$84	$63	$56
4 pairs	$112	$84	$70
5 pairs	$140	$105	$84

Page 62

1. There are 8 quarts in 2 gallons of milk.
2. There are 28 quarts in 7 gallons of milk.
3. Twenty quarts of milk equals 5 gallons.
4. She filled 2 gallons and there were 2 quarts left over.
5. The snake is 48 inches long.
6. The line was 8 feet long.

Super Challenge: The string of hot dogs was 4 whole feet with 6 inches left over.

Page 63

1. 75 feet
2. 84 inches
3. 21,120 feet
4. 360 inches
5. 297 feet

Super Challenge: 1,440 inches

Page 64

1. 48 ounces
2. 144 ounces in a 9-pound bag; 352 ounces in a 22-pound bag
3. 4 pounds
4. 168 inches
5. 40 feet

Super Challenge: Answers will vary.

Page 65

1. 2 blocks
2. 3 blocks
3. 7 blocks
4. 7 blocks
5. 4 blocks

Super Challenge: Riding up 3rd Street

Page 66

1. There are 345 miles between El Paso and Lubbock.
2. Squirmy traveled 664 miles in all.
3. Rowena traveled 75 fewer miles.
4. A round-trip would cover 708 miles.
5. The route is from San Antonio to Houston, to Dallas, to Fort Worth, to Lubbock.
6. The shortest route is from San Antonio to Austin, to Dallas, to Fort Worth, to Lubbock. The route covers 617 miles.

Super Challenge: Answers will vary.

Page 67

1. The trip is 8 miles long.
2. The trip is 12 miles long.
3. The trip is 20 miles long.
4. The shortest trip is from the Old Travel Agency, to the Old Tree, to the Old Pond. This trip is 8 miles long.
5. The trip from the Old Travel Agency to the Old Mill, Old Tree, and Old Pond covers 9 miles.

Super Challenge: Woovis started at the Old Travel Agency and went to the Old Tree, the Old Mill, and back to the Travel Agency.

Page 68

1. Judy landed in square A.
2. Down 2 squares and 4 squares to the right. Four squares to the right and down 2 squares.
3. One square to the right and 6 squares down. Six squares down and 1 square to the right.
4. Seven squares up and 5 squares to the left. Five squares to the left and 7 squares up.
5. He is 1 square down from square D.

Super Challenge: Answers will vary. Each path does not have to have the same number of squares.

Page 69

1. Rudy practiced the longest on Day 8.
2. Rudy practiced less than 5 minutes on Day 5.
3. Rudy practiced more than 45 minutes on Days 8, 9, and 11.
4. Yes.
5. Days 4 and 7
6. Less

Super Challenge: 25 minutes

Page 70

1. 5 pieces
2. 25 pieces
3. 10 pieces
4. 7 smashed pumpkins
5. 45 pieces

Super Challenge: 95 pieces

Page 71

1. 1.5 inches
2. 3.2 inches
3. The highest temperature was reached on Sunday. The lowest temperature was reached on Thursday. The difference between the two temperatures was 30 degrees.
4. The temperature dropped 15 degrees between Wednesday and Thursday. The temperature increased by 15 degrees between Saturday and Sunday.
5. 27 degrees

Super Challenge: 64 degrees

Page 72

1. Each circle stands for 1 hour.
2. Judy worked for 3 hours and 15 minutes on Monday. Judy worked 5 hours and 30 minutes on Tuesday.
3. Judy worked for 2 hours and 15 minutes more.

4. ●●●●●●◖

5. She worked for 8 hours:

●●●●●●●●

Super Challenge: Judy worked $13\frac{1}{2}$ hours:

Page 73
1. 264 inches
2. 6 inches
3. 16 inches
4. Both mirrors have the same perimeter.
5. Mirror A has a bigger perimeter than Mirror B by 2 inches.
Super Challenge: The mirror's width is 22 inches, and its perimeter is 66 inches.

Page 74
1. The perimeter is 32 inches.
2. The perimeter is 72 inches.
3. The perimeter is 13 inches.
4. The perimeter is 40 feet.
5. The perimeter is 27.5 inches.
6. The perimeter is 14.4 inches long.
Super Challenge: Each side is 12.4 inches long.

Page 75
1. The perimeter is 24 feet.
2. The area is 36 square feet.
3. The perimeter is 22 yards.
4. The perimeter is 66 feet.
5. The area is 24 square yards.
6. The length is 24 feet. The width is 9 feet.
7. The area is 216 square feet.
Super Challenge: The length is 11 yards.
The perimeter is 96 feet.

Page 76
1. A triangle
2. A square
3. A circle
4. A rectangle
5. 30 inches
Super Challenge: Answers will vary, but could include: All sides of a square are the same length. The perimeter is always 4 times the length of one side.

Page 77
1. The circumference is 37.68 inches.
2. The circumference is 75.36 inches.
3. The circumference is 12.56 feet.
4. The area is 113.04 square inches.
5. The area is 38.47 square meters.
Super Challenge: The circumference is 62.80 inches. The distance is 31.40 inches. The area is 157 square inches.

Page 78
1. 35
2. 44
3. 32
4. K, M, O
5. 352, 341, 330
Super Challenge: The wrong number is 36. The number that should replace it is 81.

Page 79
1. 3 seats
2. 6 seats
3. 6 seats
4. 1 seat
5. 2 seats
Super Challenge: 3 seats; 9 seats

Page 80
1. Moovis snores 360 times in half an hour.
2. Moovis snores 180 times in 15 minutes.
   She snores 12 times in 1 minute.
3. Harry snores 11 times in 1 minute.
4. Moovis will snore 120 more times.
5. Steve snores 840 times in 1 hour.
Super Challenge: Ant Betty snores 1,260 times in 1 hour. Ant Betty snores 420 times in 20 minutes. She snores 63 times in 3 minutes.

Page 81
1. Rudy's heart will beat 240 times in 3 minutes.
2. Rudy's heart will beat 800 times in 10 minutes, 2,400 times in 30 minutes, and 4,800 times in 1 hour.
3. Harry's heart will beat 76 times in 1 minute.
4. Harry's heart beats slower by 4 beats per minute.
5. Judy's heart beats 80 times in 1 minute and 2,400 times in half an hour.
Super Challenge: Woovis's heart beats 129,600 times in 1 day. It beats 388,800 times in 3 days. It beats 907,200 times in 1 week.

Page 82
1. Steve's wings beat 50 times in 2 seconds.
2. Steve's wings will beat 125 times.
3. Molly's wings will beat 364 times.
4. It took 8 seconds.
5. Steve's wings will beat 3,000 times.
6. It will take Steve 40 seconds.
   It will take Molly 75 seconds.
Super Challenge: Molly's wings will beat 10,800 more times.

Page 83

1. Fangella will stick out her tongue 15 times in 1 minute.
2. Fangella will stick out her tongue 45 times in 3 minutes.
3. Fangella will stick out her tongue 450 times in half an hour.
4. Fangella is 12 times longer than Squirmy.
5. She traveled 15 miles each day.

Super Challenge: Fangella collected $516. She averaged $129 per day.

Page 84

1. The car was traveling 21 miles over the speed limit.
2. Rowena was going 46 miles per hour.
3. Rowena was traveling 11 miles under the speed limit.
4. He drove 175 miles.
5. She drove 204 miles.

Super Challenge: The average mileage was 14 miles.

Page 85

1. The ratio was 1:3.
2. The ratio was 1:2.
3. Sixteen cousins were girls. The ratio was 2:1.
4. The ratio was 1:3.
5. The ratio was 4:3.
6. The ratio was 1:9.
7. The ratio was 20:1.

Super Challenge: A total of 240 ants were not hungry.

Page 86

1. BARK-RUFF, RUFF-BARK
2. You can make 2 phrases: BARK-GRR, GRR-BARK
3. You can make 6 phrases: BARK-GRR, GRR-BARK, BARK-RUFF, RUFF-BARK, GRR-RUFF, RUFF-GRR
4. You can make 6 phrases: MEOW-PURR, MEOW-SSS, PURR-SSS, PURR-MEOW, SSS-PURR, SSS-MEOW
5. You can make 6 phrases: MEOW-PURR-SSS, MEOW-SSS-PURR, PURR-MEOW-SSS, PURR-SSS-MEOW, SSS-PURR-MEOW, SSS-MEOW-PURR

Super Challenge: You can make 2 phrases: PURR-MEOW-SSS, PURR-SSS-MEOW

Page 87

1. The high score is 93. The low score is 47.
2. The range is 46.
3. 47, 73, 81, 86, 93; median score is 81.
4. 76
5. 15

Super Challenge: Answers will vary.